PACIFIC NORTHWEST LIGHTHOUSES

BY BRUCE ROBERTS *and* RAY JONES

New England Lighthouses
Bay of Fundy to Long Island Sound

Mid-Atlantic Lighthouses
Hudson River to Chesapeake Bay

Southeastern Lighthouses
Outer Banks to Cape Florida

Gulf Coast Lighthouses
Florida Keys to the Rio Grande

California Lighthouses
Point St. George to the Gulf of Santa Catalina

Pacific Northwest Lighthouses
Oregon, Washington, Alaska, and British Columbia

Western Great Lakes Lighthouses
Michigan and Superior

Eastern Great Lakes Lighthouses
Ontario, Erie, and Huron

Pacific Northwest LIGHTHOUSES

OREGON, WASHINGTON, ALASKA, *and* BRITISH COLUMBIA

PHOTOGRAPHS *by* BRUCE ROBERTS
TEXT *by* RAY JONES

CHELSEA HOUSE PUBLISHERS

Philadelphia

The lantern and powerful rotating lens of Oregon's Umpqua River Light-house.

First Chelsea House hardback edition published 2000.

All photographs, unless otherwise credited, are by Bruce Roberts.
Editorial research by Cheryl Shelton-Roberts
Cover and text design by Nancy Freeborn

Library of Congress Cataloging-in-Publication Data
Roberts, Bruce, 1930–
    Pacific Northwest lighthouses : Oregon, Washington, Alaska, and British Columbia /
photos by Bruce Roberts ; text by Ray Jones.
        p. cm. — (The lighthouse series)
    Originally published: Old Saybrook, Conn. : Globe Pequot Press, 1997.
    Includes bibliographical references and index
    Summary: Provides historical background and descriptive information on some of the most significant
lighthouses on the coast of Oregon, Washington State, British Columbia, and Alaska.
    ISBN 0-7910-5490-X (hc)
    1. Lighthouses—Northwest, Pacific. 2. Lighthouses—British Columbia. 3. Lighthouses—Alaska.
[1. Lighthouses—Northwest, Pacific—History.   2. Lighthouses—Alaska—History.]   I. Jones, Ray, 1948–
II. Title. III. Series: Lighthouse series (Philadelphia, Pa.)
VK1024.N93R93 1999
387.1'55'09795—dc21   99-26351
                                                                              CIP

Front-cover photograph: Coquille River Light, Back-cover photograph: North Head Light

Printed in Malaysia   **1 2 3 4 5 6 7 8 9 10**

For Jack Colvin, Paul Ness, Leonard Pickering, Anthony Pettit, and Dewey Dykstra;
also for my Uncle Sam, who has weathered more than a few big waves.
—*Ray Jones*

For Courtney
—*Bruce Roberts*

A golden sunset outlines the treacherous rocks of Devil's Elbow. Soon, just as it has every night since 1894, Heceta Head Lighthouse (upper right) will throw its own light out over the ocean to warn mariners of the danger.

ACKNOWLEDGMENTS

There are many people in the Canadian Coast Guard we owe thanks to. First of all, the keepers at Trial Island: Ian and Joan McNeil and Percy and Loretta Pineault. Percy picked us up at the Pedder Bay dock in Victoria and took us to Trial Island for a day of visiting with real lighthouse keepers, a fast disappearing breed. His wife, Loretta, also works in Victoria at the Coast Guard and was helpful with names and numbers that we needed. Thanks also to Mike and Carol Slater at Race Rocks, Canadian keepers with thirty years' service. Next is Chris Mills, who supplied us with many wonderful photographs of British Columbia lighthouses. He is lighthouse keeper at Ivory Island Lighthouse in Prince Rupert and an accomplished photographer. Elaine Graham provided the beautiful picture of the Atkinson Point Lighthouse, B.C. Dave Edgington, keeper at the Estevan Point Lighthouse, sent us pictures of his light, the tallest in Canada.

Thanks also to Mark Hunt of the U.S. Coast Guard in Juneau, Alaska, who supplied some wonderful images of Alaska lighthouses. Also thanks to U.S. Coast Guard Historian Robert M. Browning in Washington, D.C., who was most helpful in digging out old photos of historic lights in both Alaska and Washington. We thank Elinor DeWire, lighthouse author and photographer, who loaned us several pictures of Alaska lights. Thank you to an old friend, Jack Weil, who shared his wonderful photographs of lighthouses when weather and time prevented us from getting to certain lights.

In Crescent City, we thank Don and Carol Vestal for giving us a tour of the fascinating Battery Point Lighthouse and taking us up the tower for a memorable view of the St. George Reef Light. The Del Norte Historical Society is to be commended for restoration efforts at this light and opening it to the public to enjoy. We thank the Newport, Oregon, residents who formed the Lincoln County Historical Society and restored the old Yaquina Bay Lighthouse. Also thanks to the volunteers at Point Arena, who keep this historic light open, and who answered all our questions and were cheerful even with a cold wind blowing.

Finally, thanks to the hard-working volunteers who keep the doors open to the historic lighthouses for people to visit—and remember—all along the U.S. Northwest and Pacific Canadian coasts, such as the Mukilteo Light and Admiralty Head, Washington, and Fisgard, Victoria, B.C.

CONTENTS

Admiralty Head Lighthouse graces a glorious early evening scene on Washington's Whidbey Island. Now part of a state park, the lighthouse once served as quarters for army officers serving at nearby Fort Casey.

INTRODUCTION

Few structures speak more eloquently of the people who build and maintain them than lighthouses. Reaching far out into the night, their beacons guide ships, attract commerce, and save lives. Their warm and welcoming lights announce quite clearly that theirs are civilized shores, the home of a people who think not only of themselves but of others who may be lost in the dark. They also serve as active memorials, as reminders of all those brave souls who have gone down to the sea in ships and never returned. Of all the projects peaceful nations undertake, lighthouses must rank among the finest.

The world's first great lighthouse was also its tallest. Numbered among the Seven Wonders of the World, it was called Pharos, and it towered more than 400 feet above the harbor of the Greco-Roman city of Alexandria. Each night its keepers banked a large fire at the top of the huge tower to guide trading ships into the harbor. The purpose of Pharos was to serve commerce, and this it did well for more than 1,000 years.

Commerce was also what George Washington had in mind—the dollar bill really is a fitting tribute to the man—when he made the construction of lighthouses a priority of his presidency. Under pressure from Washington, Congress set up the "Lighthouse Establishment" in 1789 as one of its first official acts under the Constitution. As with ancient Pharos, most of America's early lighthouses were intended to guide seagoing freighters and their money-making cargoes into port. Partly because their lighthouses served this purpose so well, cities like Boston and New York became bustling, world-class commercial centers.

It would have been difficult for members of the nation's first Congress to imagine that the dozen or so wood and stone towers they commissioned would eventually be part of a system of hundreds of lighthouses and thousands of lesser navigational aides. Within little more than a century, America's lighthouse system would protect more than 12,000 miles of coastline. By 1904 the nation's westernmost light station would stand on improbably remote Unimak Island, almost one quarter of the globe away from the old East Coast.

LIGHTS *on the* LAST FRONTIER

The Northwest is the last frontier for North American lighthouses and their keepers. To those who have traveled extensively in Oregon, Washington, British Columbia, and Alaska, this bold and breathtaking region, larger in area than all but a few entire nations, is often known as the *Great* Northwest. Although the region is also great in terms of resources, for many years lighthouse construction here lagged behind that on other U.S. and Canadian coasts. This was true partly because settlement in this region came later than elsewhere. Populations were less dense, so that northwestern communities often lacked the votes to pressure their governments into action. At the same time, with more than 8,000 miles of coastline, as rugged and dangerous as it is beautiful, the Northwest presented the U.S. and Canadian governments with an almost impossible task.

Following a flurry of lighthouse construction in the mid-1800s, efforts to mark northwestern shipping lanes declined. At many points along the coast, sometimes for stretches of a hundred miles or more, captains were in the dark and on their own. Although hundreds of ships and thousands of lives were lost in wrecks that might have been prevented, little was done to make these threatening shores safer. With the rapid growth of the northwestern fishing industry late in the nineteenth century and the discovery of gold in the Klondike in 1896, government purse strings began to loosen—but only gradually. Then came the wreck of the passenger steamer *Valencia* off Vancouver Island in 1906. Few events before or since have done so much to change public or government attitudes toward shipping safety.

GHOST SHIP *of the* GREAT NORTHWEST

She glides cloudlike over the ocean surface as if the pitching swells could not reach her hull, as if she floated, not on the water, but on mist. Frozen in the rigging above her decks hang human forms, their limbs stiff, their faces expressionless, their voices silent. The ship is silent, too. There are no throbbing engines, no creaking lines, no rattling chains. Whenever the *Valencia* appears in a dense shroud of northwestern fog, she is seen but never heard. And no sooner is she seen than she vanishes into the same dark hideaway from which she came, a place where no seaman would ever choose to follow. The *Valencia* comes and goes like the fog itself.

Phantom ships such as the *Valencia* and the fabled *Flying Dutchman* are the stuff of sea yarns spun in the pubs and saloons of ports the world over. The quality of a seaman's story often depends on the quantity of the beverage remaining in his mug, but its truthfulness is never in doubt. The fact is that most such tales, even if a trifle embellished, are rooted in historical incidents, some of them even more grizzly and frightening than the ghostly stories they have spawned. In the case of the *Valencia*, the truth *is* the horror.

JANUARY 20, 1906

The boiler fires in the *Valencia's* belly roared as Captain O. M. Johnson ordered steam brought up to full pressure. Burly crewmen threw off the heavy hemp hawsers, and the 1,598-ton Pacific Coast Company liner eased away from Meiggs Wharf in San Francisco to begin its regularly scheduled run to Victoria, British Columbia.

Nearly every one of the *Valencia's* 154 passengers stood on deck to bid a fond farewell to friends, family, and the city by the bay. Among those waving from the shore were Captain Johnson's wife and small daughter, who stood in the bay window of their modest harborside apartment. This was not an unusually tearful parting for the Johnson family. A twelve-year company veteran, the captain had made this journey many times. There was every reason to believe that this trip would be as uneventful as past ones and that he would return in a few days, perhaps with a bag of candy and bit of lace from Canada.

This trip would not be like the others, however. As the *Valencia* steamed toward the entrance of the bay, an ominous midday fog poured through the Golden Gate Strait from the ocean. Drawing like a veil between the ship and the shore, it obscured the view of passengers who strained to catch one last glimpse of the city. Most of them would never see it again.

In fact, the city they knew and loved would, itself, soon disappear forever. A little less than three months after the *Valencia* steamed out of its harbor for the last time, earthquake and fire would sweep away gracious old Victorian San Francisco. A modern and very different city would replace it.

Captain Johnson and his crew had pushed through countless Pacific fogs, some so dense that a man could barely see his own hand when held at arm's length, but never one as thick and stubborn as this. For hour after hour, all day long and throughout the next, the fog held the *Valencia* in its blinding grip. To navigate, the captain was forced to rely on compass headings and charts. By keeping careful track of the ship's speed, he could accurately plot his position—or so he thought. Although he understood that this sort of navigation was guesswork, Johnson trusted his experience, his instincts, and his ability to navigate by dead reckoning. All it took was hard work, a professional seaman's careful attention to detail, and just a touch of luck. Allowing himself little sleep, he kept close by the helm, poring over his charts, making his calculations, and always refiguring them.

JANUARY 22, 1906

After more than two days of plowing steadily northward along the coasts of Oregon and Washington, the *Valencia* had reached Cape Flattery and the Strait of Juan de Fuca. At least, that is what Johnson's charts indicated, and that is what he believed. Because of the fog, he could not verify the ship's position. There was no sign of the Cape Flattery Light, the Umatilla Reef Lightship, or any other familiar seamark. There was only the fog and the nasty gale that had blown in from the Pacific to join it. So the captain had his men take soundings. He knew that near the strait, the ocean's depth would drop off precipitously. Once he had 150 fathoms or more under his ship's keel, he could turn confidently toward the east, the calmer waters of Juan de Fuca, and safe harbor at Victoria.

The first depth reading Captain Johnson received was one of "sixty fathoms." Shortly afterwards he heard his men call out "fifty fathoms," and then "thirty fathoms!" Instead of dropping away to the abysmal depths he had expected, the sea floor was rushing up toward him.

"Where are we?" he asked. It was a rhetorical question, one the other officers on the bridge made no attempt to answer.

Increasingly alarmed, the captain rang the engine room and ordered "half speed," and then "dead slow." Now barely moving forward, the *Valencia* wallowed late into the evening through the swells. "Where are we?" the captain grumbled.

Johnson and his men had reason to believe they would very soon know the answer to that all-important question. To their considerable relief, they had begun to see torn patches of clear sky. At last the fog was beginning to break, but as it did, the ominous dark shapes of sawtoothed rocks could be seen off the starboard bow.

Suddenly, one of those rocks loomed dead ahead. Immediately, the order was given for "full stop!" and "hard to starboard!" but it was too late. Passengers and crew could all hear the stomach-wrenching sound of metal grinding over stone.

"In the name of God, where are we?" shouted Captain Johnson. In fact, he and the *Valencia* were just off Pachena Point, well to the north of the Strait of Juan de Fuca and almost a hundred miles northwest of Victoria. The Japanese current had pushed the *Valencia* along faster than its captain had reckoned. Each time he marked off twenty nautical miles on the chart with his caliper, the *Valencia* had actually steamed twenty-two or even twenty-three miles northward. Finally, the inevitable had happened, and she had nicked her

Originally intended for nearby Foulweather Cape, this tower was mistakenly built on Oregon's lovely but threatening Yaquina Head. Its 93-foot-tall Italianate tower and first-order lens have served mariners since 1873.

bow on the long, sharp blade of Vancouver Island. Now she was trapped in a maze of ship-killing rocks.

The first impact was not fatal, but soon the *Valencia* slammed into another rock and ripped a gaping hole in her iron hull. A flood of seawater flushed the stokers from the engine room, sending everyone belowdecks scrambling up the ladders. Determined to avoid sinking in deep water, the doomed liner's captain turned his ship toward the breakers, and the *Valencia* made one last desperate lunge for shore. She had gotten within thirty yards of a cobblestone beach before she lurched to a stop and stuck fast in the shallows. It was now just after midnight.

JANUARY 23, 1906

Having run aground, the *Valencia* had been saved, temporarily at least, from sinking, but she remained fully exposed to a merciless sea. Towering, storm-driven waves roared out of the darkness, pounding her amidships and threatening to tear her apart. It was impossible to tell how long she would last.

Rising water had driven the panic-stricken passengers onto the upper decks, where Captain Johnson and his officers struggled to maintain order. The *Valencia* had plenty of lifeboats, and in less violent conditions, they could have been used to ferry everyone across the few dozen yards of surf that separated them from safety. But each attempt to launch a boat met with disaster. The first boat sent into the water promptly overturned, spilling two crewmen and a dozen or more women and children into the surf, where they drowned or were crushed by the rocks. The next attempt to launch a boat had the same tragic result.

Meanwhile, with monotonous regularity, the huge breakers poured over the decks, sweeping away screaming passengers. Again, it was most often the women and children who fell victim to the waves and were dragged overboard into the freezing water. To escape the waves, some climbed into the rigging, where they quickly froze to death and fell back onto the deck with a sickening thud.

Firing signal flares in hopes of drawing attention to the *Valencia*'s plight, Captain Johnson had a rocket explode in his hand, blowing off two of his fingers. He calmly tied a rag around the mangled hand and continued his efforts to save his passengers and crew. At daybreak he order the ship's Lyle gun into action, firing tethered harpoons toward land. If a line could be secured in this way, people could roll across it to safety in a sort of cart called a breeches-buoy. Unfortunately, none of the harpoons took hold.

During the previous night two more boats had been sent into the water. Both were thrown over by the waves, but several men aboard one of the boats managed to reach shore. At dawn they set out across the wild country. Eventually, they reached a telegraph shack, where they sent

The octagonal concrete tower of the Point Wilson Lighthouse marks the entrance to strategic Admiralty Inlet. The fixed white light flashes red every few seconds.

word of the disaster to Victoria. Several relief ships raced to Pachena Point, but when they reached the wreck, they found there was nothing they could do to help the survivors still trapped aboard the *Valencia*. The seas had not calmed in the least, and it was impossible to reach the wreck in a small boat. The would-be rescuers could only watch in horror as the *Valencia* began to fall apart.

With the hull of his ship breaking up under him, Captain Johnson ordered his last two lifeboats into the water. By his command, the boats were to be filled with the ship's surviving women—pitifully, no children now remained alive aboard the *Valencia*. However, no amount of pleading could coax the women into the boats. Having time and again seen bodies torn to pieces in the surf, they all refused to leave the dying ship. Unable to convince the women to make the attempt to save themselves, Captain Johnson decided to remain with them and see the *Valencia* through its last minutes. He knew this meant

A sleek Washington State ferry passes Mukilteo Lighthouse with its century-old Fresnel lens. Despite its age, the French-made lens does its job better than most "modern" navigational aids.

he would never see his wife and daughter again, but at the moment, these frightened women *were* his family. As the last great waves were about to blast the *Valencia*, breaking the ship and the people on board into unrecognizable pieces, Captain Johnson led his passengers in the old hymn "Nearer My God to Thee."

BRIGHT LEGACY *of the* VALENCIA

Only thirty-seven passengers and crew survived the wreck of the *Valencia*. At least 117 others perished. Readers in the United States, Canada, and throughout the world quickly learned of their terrible fate as newspapers and magazines served up the *Valencia* tragedy in gruesome detail. A classic adventure story, it was the sort of tale that sold newsprint. It featured a doomed liner loaded with passengers and lost in the fog, a losing battle against the overwhelming forces of nature, a heroic crew struggling in vain to save their ship, and a brave captain who made all the wrong decisions for all the right reasons and who, in the end, decided to go down with his ship. It even closed with a hymn.

Ironically, this was the same hymn—"Nearer My God to Thee"—that would be sung just six years later aboard the *Titanic* as she slipped down into the icy North Atlantic. The sinking of the *Titanic* has been described as "the news story of the century." Even so, the loss of the *Titanic* could hardly have had more influence on maritime history and government policy toward shipping safety than that of the *Valencia*.

The *Valencia* story had one especially compelling element, namely, a *lighthouse* that might have saved the little liner except that it had never been built. The Canadian government had long considered establishing a light station atop the cliffs at Pachena Point, overlooking the very rocks that ripped open the *Valencia*'s hull. Had such a light existed on the night of January 22, 1906, Captain Johnson might have seen it and turned his ship away. But in 1906 there was no light on Pachena Point. Faced with the same budget constraints and competing priorities that decision makers in Ottawa and Washington are still forced to wrestle with today, Canadian officials had put off the project year after year.

The public outcry over the *Valencia* tragedy forced the U.S. and Canadian governments to pour more resources into their lighthouse services. Dozens of new lights were established and older ones

Built in 1906, the wooden Mukilteo Lighthouse looks old-fashioned, but its beacon remains vital to navigation. The 30-foot octagonal tower contains a small but powerful fourth-order Fresnel lens.

improved and refitted. Whereas commerce had long been the primary determining factor in the selection of sites for lighthouses and other navigational aids, new emphasis was now placed on the safety of ships, crews, and passengers. All of this activity was of particular benefit to the Northwest, which had previously stood near the bottom of the list when it came to public expenditures. Of special note, the long-delayed Pachena Lighthouse was completed and in service by the spring of 1908 (see chapter three), less than eighteen months after Captain Johnson's ship struck Vancouver Island.

Today the once-dark coast of the Northwest sparkles with lights. Shining every night and always in fog or heavy weather, they serve as an active memorial to the victims of the *Valencia* tragedy and to the thousands of other mariners who have lost their lives along these dangerous coasts. They also continue to perform an all-important service. No one will ever know how many ships and lives these lights have saved. History rarely takes note of accidents that do not happen.

Nowadays well-equipped vessels are guided by precise navigational information supplied via satellite and sophisticated radar. But when it comes to the safety of a ship, its passengers, and crew, captains are likely to fall back on the old ways. That is why every night, from Coos Bay, Oregon, to Unimak Island in the Aleutians, ship's masters are seen peering out into the darkness searching for a light on the horizon.

This book tells the story of the Northwest's most important and historic lighthouses. Wherever possible, readers are given travel information so that they can visit and experience the old lighthouses for themselves. *Northwestern Lighthouses* is the most recent in a series of seven books by the same authors celebrating the North American Lighthouse tradition. For other titles in the series, check your local bookstore or contact Globe Pequot Press at (800) 243–0495.

CHAPTER ONE

Lights of
THE ROCKY SHORES
OREGON

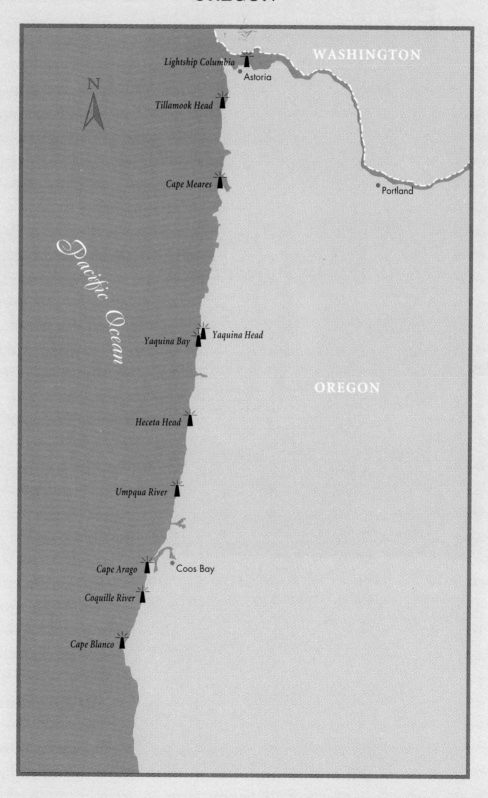

Visitors examine the big, first-order Fresnel lens at northern Oregon's now inactive Cape Meares Lighthouse. Unfortunately, the old lens has been damaged by vandals. Fresnels are so expensive and intricately constructed that they are considered irreplaceable.

*A*s an outpost of human endeavor, the Tillamook Rock Lighthouse was always as much a symbol as a navigational aid. It marked not only a dangerous maritime hazard but also the precarious and shifting border between human enterprise and the forces of nature.

Located more than a mile offshore, near Oregon's magnificent Tillamook Head and about twenty miles south of the Columbia River, this storm-dashed bastion clings to a scrap of rock almost totally in the grip of the sea. In a gale, mountainous waves sweep over the rock and pound the walls of the lighthouse. Few buildings anywhere in the world are so exposed to the whims and power of wind, weather, and sea. Yet the Tillamook Rock Lighthouse has stood now, more or less intact, for more than a century.

A TOEHOLD *on the* ROCK

Completed early in 1881, the structure surely ranks among the foremost engineering triumphs of the late nineteenth century. But there were many who said the lighthouse could never be built. In fact, the public took such a skeptical view of the project, there was a general outcry against wasting tax money on so vain and foolish a venture.

Well before the first stone was laid, tragedy threatened to convert public opposition to outrage. A master mason from Portland with previous experience in building seemingly unbuildable lighthouses, John Trewavas was put ashore on the rock one morning in September 1879. Trewavas had been asked to survey the site, but he never even got started. While climbing up the rock's sheer eastern face, he slipped and plunged into the sea. The water immediately closed over him, and he was never seen again.

News of the mason's death raised such a storm of protest that government officials felt they could only proceed with the project in secret. The construction crew chosen for the job was sequestered and housed in an isolated location.

Even some of the workmen—several were tough veterans of other dangerous construction projects—questioned the wisdom of attempting to build on this sea-battered outcropping. The task before them was indeed Olympian. The first two workmen put ashore on the rock became so frightened by the giant waves crashing into it that they jumped into the sea and had to be rescued by lifeline.

Finally, the crew got a foothold when, on October 21, 1879, the revenue cutter *Corwin* landed four workers, along with provisions, blankets, water, and a few tools. These four pioneers were in for a hard time. Soon a gale blew up, driving away the *Corwin* and leaving them marooned. Waves broke completely over the rock, shaking loose huge boulders and terrifying the drenched and generally miserable workers. Over the next few days, the *Corwin* made repeated attempts to approach the rock, but the horrible weather always sent the cutter scurrying back for safe harbor in the Columbia River.

Firmly in the grip of the Pacific, Tillamook Rock was probably the most remote and least hospitable light station in America. Its construction was a heroic feat, and keeping the station supplied required fortitude. Here supplies are sent across on a cable from a Coast Guard tender. (Courtesy U.S. Coast Guard)

At last, more than a week after the first landing, the *Corwin* renewed contact with the rock and its bedraggled inhabitants. But instead of rescuing them, it put ashore five more workers, along with construction superintendent M. A. Ballantyne. Obviously, this job required more than the usual measure of fortitude and determination.

Within a few days the crew had anchored their tools and supplies, built themselves a crude, fortresslike barracks designed to resist the ocean's insistent pounding, and set to work blasting and chiseling a level foundation for the lighthouse. All through the winter and spring the work continued. On more than one occasion gales with hurricane-force winds threatened to blow or wash the little crew off the rock, but they gritted their teeth and held on. And when the winds died down again, they returned to the business of cutting and blasting stone.

By the end of May the rock's pointed crown had been lopped off, making way for the foundation of a lighthouse. On June 17 a lighthouse tender arrived with a load of fine-grained basalt construction stone, and less than a week afterwards, the cornerstone was laid. Six months later the last of the mortar had dried, fixing firmly in place the stones in the combination light tower and dwelling. By New Year's Day 1881, the station's enormous first-order Fresnel lens was being installed meticulously, one delicate prism at a time. Later that day a tremendous gale blew in, bring the work to a complete, though temporary, halt.

As this photograph suggests, keepers had to risk their lives to get on and off Tillamook Rock—especially in bad weather. (Courtesy National Archives)

That night workers on the rock began to hear strange noises above the roar of the storm. They thought they heard voices, men calling to them from the darkness. They also heard, quite distinctly, a dog barking. Suddenly, out of the gloom, a large sailing ship came into sight. It reeled and crashed over the waves, obviously out of control. Then, as quickly as it had appeared, the ship was gone.

A day later, when the storm had passed and the sun came out, the fate of the mystery ship and its crew became all too apparent. Its shattered remains littered the rocks of nearby Tillamook Head. The unlucky ship had been the *Lupatia,* bound from Japan to the Columbia River. None of its crew of sixteen lived to tell the story of the destruction. Only the ship's dog survived.

The *Lupatia* calamity provided a somber initiation for the almost-complete Tillamook Rock Lighthouse. No doubt the disaster chilled and depressed the construction crew. After all their struggles they had missed by only a few days having the light ready and shining on the night when it was most needed by the *Lupatia.*

The oil lamp inside the big Fresnel lens was fired up for the first time on January 11, 1881. The light shined almost continuously for the next seventy-six years. It was finally extinguished in September 1957, when the lighthouse was decommissioned and replaced by a buoy.

The lighthouse was never automated and during its active years was always manned. The keepers of the Tillamook Rock Lighthouse lived an isolated and lonely existence, even by the standards of their profession. They were often exposed to the worst insults the ocean could throw at them. On the darkest and stormiest nights, they inevitably grew weary of their rock and questioned their choice of work. Perhaps, to renew their commitment, they sometimes stood in the lantern room and remembered the tragic story of the *Lupatia.* It is easy to imagine that on such occasions, when the wind died down and the foghorn was silent, they could hear a dog barking.

CAPE BLANCO LIGHT

Port Oxford, Oregon – 1870

The southernmost of Oregon's major lights is Cape Blanco. The fifty-nine-foot conical tower stands far up on the rocks of the cape, which raises the focal plane of the second-order Fresnel lens to a lofty 245 feet above mean sea level. As a result, Cape Blanco is Oregon's highest light. Its one-million-candlepower flashes can be seen from twenty-two miles at sea.

The light station takes its name from the cape's precipitous white cliffs, which drop down almost vertically to the beaches below. Seen from out at sea, the cliffs are quite beautiful, especially when evening sunlight washes them with color. Mariners seldom take the time to appreciate their beauty, however, for these are among the most dangerous waters in America.

(Photo by John W. Weil)

Countless vessels have piled up on the rocks along this treacherous stretch of coast. In 1883 the steamer *Victoria* foundered on the reefs off Cape Blanco. Six years later the sidewheeler *Alaskan* broke up and sank within sight of the lighthouse. Down with her went thirty of her forty-seven passengers and crew. In 1895 the 1,430-ton British steamer *Bawnmore*, carrying, of all things, a cargo of streetcars, went ashore a few miles north of the light. A fast-working lifesaving team saved the passengers and crew, but most of the streetcars were lost. No one is sure what happened to the steam schooner *South Coast*, which disappeared off Cape Blanco during a late-summer storm in 1930. Carrying a heavy load of cedar logs from California, the schooner vanished, along with her entire crew of nineteen. Later the schooner's deckhouse washed ashore on the cape.

Government officials were well aware of the dangers of the cape when they commissioned construction of the lighthouse in 1868. They paid $20,000 for its powerful eight-sided, first-order Fresnel lens, which was handmade in Paris under the direction of famed lens maker Henry Lapaute. The huge lens was replaced many years ago by a second-order revolving lens seven feet high and five feet in diameter. Placed in service in December 1870, it began to warn sailors away from the cape's ship-killing rocks and reefs. Before that time mariners had to rely on their instincts and their lucky stars to get them safely past the rocks, although they sometimes got a little help from a friendly innkeeper named Louis Knapp. In harsh weather and in the winter, Knapp always kept a lantern burning in the window of his hotel near the cape. Sailors learned to look for it.

Perhaps Knapp deserves to be known as the first lighthouse keeper in this area. But its best-known keeper was surely James Langlois, who came to Cape Blanco in 1875. With the help of two female assistants, Langlois kept the light burning for forty-two years.

HOW TO GET THERE:

The lighthouse is located near Cape Blanco State Park off Highway 101, a few miles north of Port Orford. Visitors can walk the grounds around the tower. The light is best viewed from the beach.

COQUILLE RIVER LIGHT

Bandon, Oregon – 1896

Now an attraction of Bullards Beach State Park, this little lighthouse stood empty and ignored for nearly half a century—longer, in fact, than it served as an active light station. Gutted by vandals after the Coast Guard abandoned it in 1939, it was left to deteriorate—a sorry end for a structure that saved so many ships from destruction in the treacherous shallows of the Coquille River.

In 1870 the schooner *Commodore* ran aground and broke up on the bar near the entrance of the river. Since that first wreck the list of the Coquille's victims has grown long and impressive. It includes many schooners, such as the *Randolph* (lost in 1915), the *E. L. Smith* (sunk in 1935), and the *Golden Way* (foundered in 1936), as well as a large number of tugs and other vessels. Three schooners, the *Onward*, *Western Homer*, and *Del Norte*, went down here in little more than a year, between 1904 and 1905.

Most of these unfortunate vessels came to the Coquille River to take on loads of lumber harvested from Oregon's tall virgin forests. Late in the last century, the lumber traffic in and out of the riverside port of Bandon became brisk, and sea captains demanded a light to help them navigate the Coquille's treacherous entrance. The

As romantically inspiring as a full moon, the restored Coquille River Lighthouse paints a bright streak over the water. This photograph was taken from Bandon, on the opposite bank of the Coquille River, with a telephoto lens.

bar at the mouth of the river was considered by many among the most dangerous on the West Coast.

Completed in 1895, the forty-foot lighthouse tower was made of brick protected by a layer of stucco. It was given a relatively small, fourth-order Fresnel lens. First lighted in 1896, it burned for more than four decades before it was abandoned and replaced by a series of buoys and a small jetty light.

Oregon boasts one of the most extensive and varied park systems in the country, as evidenced by this peaceful scene at Bullards Beach State Park near Bandon. The Coquille River Lighthouse stands in the distance.

HOW TO GET THERE:

Located in Bullards Beach State Park off Highway 101 near Bandon, the lighthouse has been carefully restored and is open daily during the summer. Just across the river in Bandon are several restaurants and the Lighthouse Inn, all offering excellent views of the light.

CAPE ARAGO LIGHT

Charleston, Oregon – 1934

Another seamark familiar to lumber freighters is the Cape Arago Lighthouse, located less than two miles southwest of the entrance to Coos Bay. For almost one and a half centuries, ships have sailed into the bay to take on loads of lumber and wood products. Even today the city of Coos Bay and its sister city, North Bend, are often fragrant with the aroma of freshly sawn wood. Oregon's forests still provide much of the commerce in this region, which was once known to people in the forest industry as "the softwood capital of the world."

By the time of the Civil War, Coos Bay already attracted enough seagoing traffic to require a lighthouse. In 1866 a light station was established on a small, strategically placed island just north of Cape Arago. From here it could guide ships into the bay and also serve as a marker for vessels passing up and down the Oregon coast.

The original iron tower stood for more than four decades before erosion forced the Lighthouse Board to replace it. A wooden structure built further back from the rapidly weathering cliffs, the station's second lighthouse

The fourth-order lens of the Cape Arago Lighthouse shines through a thin fog. The light serves Coos Bay, famous as a lumber port.

served for only thirty years before it, too, was threatened by erosion. Completed in 1934, a third lighthouse, built of reinforced concrete, has proved more durable than its predecessors.

It still stands, more than half a century after its construction, although its island perch is considerably diminished. Wind and weather are constantly cutting away the island, which is connected to the mainland by a narrow footbridge.

The octagonal concrete tower is forty-four feet tall, and together with the elevation of the island, places the fourth-order light about one hundred feet above mean sea level, making it visible from approximately sixteen miles at sea. The light is a welcome sight to mariners, for this stretch of the Oregon coast is among the rockiest and most dangerous passages for ships in American waters.

Wind and water have separated the lighthouse from the mainland. The iron footbridge shown in the foreground provides access.

HOW TO GET THERE:

Cape Arago and its lighthouse stand about 2 miles south of Charleston, which is located inside the entrance to Coos Bay. To reach Charleston, turn west off Highway 101 at the city of Coos Bay. The lighthouse is not open to the public.

UMPQUA RIVER LIGHT

Winchester Bay, Oregon – 1894

The conical, plaster-covered masonry tower of the Umpqua River Lighthouse rises above the treetops of a state park named in its honor. Lush bracken grows beneath the soughing branches. Beyond are acres of sand dunes, golden-hued beaches, and the expanse of Winchester Bay.

At night the flashing light, alternating red and white, can be seen from twenty-one miles away. Coos Bay lies nineteen miles to the south, within range of the beacon. The peaceful setting contrasts sharply with the violent and often tragic history of this stretch of coast.

The original lighthouse was erected in 1857 to mark the entrance of the Umpqua River and warn mariners of a shifting sandbar that had wrecked at least six vessels between 1850 and 1855. The tower was the first of its kind in Oregon.

As solid as the day it was built, the Umpqua River Lighthouse has stood since 1894. An earlier tower, built in 1857, collapsed after a storm weakened its foundation.

From the moment they began laying the foundation, the construction crew was pestered by Indians who made repeated attempts, sometimes successful, to steal tools, supplies, and whatever valuables they could lay their hands on. Relations with the local Indians had once been friendly, but they became increasingly strained. Open hostilities were avoided when a construction foreman set off a stick of dynamite. The Indians had never heard such a frightful explosion, and they scattered into the surrounding forests.

Nature provided a more formidable enemy for the lighthouse than the Indians had been for its builders. Only four years after it was completed, the foundation was undercut by floods and surf, and the tower collapsed into the river. Despite nearly constant lobbying by Oregon legislators and the shipping industry, Congress refused to appropriate funds for a new lighthouse until well into the 1890s. Eventually, the loss of vessels such as the schooner *Sparrow*, which went down with three crew members at the entrance of the river, forced the government to act.

Completed in 1894, the present sixty-five-foot tower was crowned with a powerful, first-order Fresnel lens. The site, well above the river, raises the focal plane of the light 165 feet above the sea. The flashing light reduced shipping losses, but it often proved no match for the thick fog of the Pacific Northwest. For instance, a pair of coastal freighters, the *Admiral Nicholson* and the *G. C. Lindauer*, came ashore a short distance from the light on the night of May 16, 1924. A pasty fog had enveloped the area that night and blocked the view of the light.

Not all of those who have moored their lives temporarily or permanently off the coast of Oregon have done so to assist mariners, to fish, or to carry on the commerce of the sea. As with all of the earth's environments, the ocean sometimes attracts evil. On the sea, evil often takes the name of piracy.

One usually thinks of pirates as a swashbuckling, eye-patched denizens of the Barbary coast or of the Caribbean during the age of Spanish treasure galleons and the gold doubloon. But there have been pirates in every age and on every shore, even the rocky coast of Oregon.

On the night of August 21, 1909, Oregon's Umpqua River Light could be seen flashing in the distance by the crew of the Alaska Pacific Navigation Company liner *Buckman* as she plied through the ocean about twenty miles offshore. Outward bound from Seattle, she was about to be under siege by a pair of twentieth-century pirates.

The pirates, George Washington Wise and French West, a former sailor, had boarded the vessel in Seattle. Now, shortly before midnight, they stealthily approached the bridge.

Armed with a shotgun and a pistol, the pair had a gruesome plan. They intended to kill the crew, run the vessel aground near the Umpqua River, and then make off with a shipment of gold they believed to be aboard. The ship's passengers would be left to save themselves as best they could.

From the bridge wing the armed pirates burst into the pilothouse. There Wise held the ship's officer and helmsman hostage while his accomplice went aft to rouse Captain Edwin Wood, who was asleep in his cabin. As the ship's startled skipper groped for his revolver in the darkened cabin, West killed him with a shotgun blast.

The shot alarmed Wise, who ran from the pilothouse. No longer facing Wise's cocked pistol, the helmsman hurriedly gave the alarm by repeatedly pulling the ship's whistle cord.

The crew poured onto the deck, and in the ensuing confusion, First Officer Richard Brennan slipped into the captain's cabin. There he found the captain's revolver; he then hurried to the pilothouse, where he wounded West in a shootout. The bloodied pirate leapt over the side into the darkness, never to be seen again.

Later Wise was found cowering belowdecks. The crew clamped him in irons and, when the ship reached port, turned him over to the authorities. Eventually, he was sent to an asylum for the criminally insane.

The *Buckman* had not been carrying gold that night.

HOW TO GET THERE:

The Umpqua River Lighthouse can be seen from the adjacent Umpqua Lighthouse State Park. The park is located off Highway 101, just south of Winchester Bay.

HECETA HEAD LIGHT

Florence, Oregon – 1894

In 1755, the year the American Revolution began, Captain Don Bruno de Heceta of the Spanish Royal Navy led an expedition along the largely unknown coast of the Pacific Northwest. An explorer in the service of the king of Spain, Heceta charted scores of craggy outcroppings reaching far out into the sea from the mainland. Heceta was among the first Europeans to look in wonder at the magnificent headland rising sharply out of the sea about eleven miles north of the mouth of the Siuslaw River. Today that headland bears his name. So, too, does its lighthouse, one of the most beautiful and storied navigational markers in America.

Before 1894 there had been no light to guide ships along the ninety miles between Cape Foulweather and Cape Arago. The crews of ships plying the waters off this stretch of coast were left to find their way in the dark. But in the spring of that year, a fifty-six-foot-tall white masonry tower was completed high up on the Heceta Head cliffs, and a bright light began to shine from its lantern.

To build the lighthouse in this remote location had taken nearly two years and $180,000—a fantastic sum at the time. Construction materials had to be brought in by ship and barge to the nearby Siuslaw River and then hauled in mule-drawn wagons to the foot of the headland. Construction stone from the Clackamas River near Oregon City was carried to the site by the lighthouse tender *Columbine*. Bricks and cement were shipped from San Francisco and reloaded onto barges at Florence, to be towed up the Siuslaw by the tugboat *Lillian*. Lumber, most of it from Oregon mills, was unloaded at the river

With its simple design, stark white walls, and red trim, the delightful Heceta Head Lighthouse shows why some think it the most beautiful lighthouse in the West—or anywhere. (Photo by John W. Weil)

and rafted to a cove below Heceta Head.

The new lighthouse was fitted with an exquisite first-order Fresnel lens supplied by Chance Brothers of London. Its 640 prisms of finely molded glass were as clear as a beaker of spring water.

Light came from a five-wick coal-oil lamp. A weighted cable attached to a series of gears turned the lamp, causing the light to flash. The weight reached bottom every four hours and had to be pulled up again by the keeper or one of his two assistants. The chief keeper and his family lived in a house some distance from the tower, while his assistants lived in a second house nearby.

In 1910 the original apparatus was replaced by a gas-type bunsen burner, which in turn was replaced by an electric light. Today, a 1.1-million-candlepower bulb burns in the Heceta Head lantern. The old, but still highly efficient, lens gathers the light and concentrates it into a narrow beam that can be seen from twenty-one miles away. Because of the height of its perch on the Heceta Cliffs, the lighthouse sends its beam seaward from an elevation of 205 feet.

Electric power for the light station is supplied by a local utility company, but the Coast Guard maintains an auxiliary system to keep the light burning in case of outages. During nearly a century of service, the light has failed only once, in 1961, when a mud slide temporarily cut electric cables.

HOW TO GET THERE:

One of the most photographed lighthouses on the West Coast, the Heceta Head Light Station stands on a craggy point about 11 miles north of Florence. Although the grounds are open to the public, the lighthouse itself is closed. Some of the best views of the lighthouse can be had from Highway 101 south of Heceta Head, Devils Elbow State Park, and the beach below the head.

Perched on its ocean cliff, the Heceta Head Lighthouse is even more lovely from a distance.

YAQUINA BAY LIGHT

Newport, Oregon – 1871

Built of wood instead of brick and stone, like most of its cousin along the Pacific coast, the white-frame Yaquina Bay Lighthouse has nonetheless stood the test of time. Recently restored, it remains today in excellent condition almost one and a quarter centuries after it was commissioned. Its durability is all the more remarkable considering that its light was put out in 1874 after one of history's shortest terms of active service for any lighthouse.

Built on the crest of a hill at the north entrance of Yaquina Bay, it was lighted on November 3, 1871. Less than three years later its lantern went dark, the victim of a bureaucratic bungle. The Lighthouse Board had set aside funds for construction of another lighthouse at Cape Foulweather, well to the north of Yaquina Bay. When the construction materials arrived in the fall of 1872, however, they were mistakenly landed at the headland, little more than three miles from the already

Rendered superfluous by its neighbor on Yaquina Head, the Yaquina Bay Lighthouse was active for only three years (1871–74). Fortunately for lovers of lighthouse lore and unique architecture, the handsome structure still stands. Note the small red lantern protruding through the roof.

operating Yaquina Bay Lighthouse. Construction crews quickly rendered the mistake into stone by throwing up a fine tower in only a few months.

By the time the unnecessary Yaquina Head station was complete and ready for use, officials realized that they now had one more lighthouse than was needed to serve the area properly. As a result, the smaller and less powerful Yaquina Bay Light was discontinued. Its whale-oil lamps were extinguished and its fifth-order Fresnel lens winked out on October 1, 1874.

People might have supposed at the time that the abandoned wooden structure would soon be demolished. Not so. The building eventually was put to use as a crew station for the U.S. Lifesaving Service. The hardy surfmen lived in the old lighthouse and used it as a lookout for vessels negotiating the bar.

By the 1940s the weather-beaten building had become dilapidated, and there was talk of razing it. But the Lincoln County Historical Society fought and won the battle to save it. The handsome wooden edifice with its shuttered windows serves today as a tourist attraction and museum. Some believe the building is haunted. Rumor has it that during the 1930s, a visitor disappeared without a trace.

Inside the Yaquina Bay Lighthouse, simple furnishings recall earlier days.

HOW TO GET THERE:

The Yaquina Bay Lighthouse has been inactive for more than a century but is well worth a visit. The Friends of Yaquina Bay Lighthouse and the U.S. Forestry Department maintain the structure as a museum. It is filled with nineteenth-century furnishings and artifacts, including rope beds, kerosene lamps, pewter cutlery, and hand water pumps. The museum is open daily. Its hours are 12:00–5:00 P.M. Memorial Day through September 30 and 12:00–4:00 P.M. the remainder of the year.

YAQUINA HEAD LIGHT

Newport, Oregon – 1873

One of the most beautiful lighthouses in America, the Yaquina Head Light is a magnet for photographers and tourists, who can see it from U.S. 101, the Pacific Coast Highway. The magnificent rock outcropping on which the light station stands is a magnet of a more literal variety. At its core is a rich vein of magnetized iron that raises cain with the compasses of ships passing nearby.

Most vessels sailing up and down the Oregon coast give this headland a wide berth, but not just because it makes their compasses dance. Numerous ships have come to grief along this stretch of coast, many of them within sight of the lighthouse. Some met their ends on the reefs off the headland itself. Long ago, the lighthouse builders carved footholds into the stony cliffs so that shipwrecked

The Yaquina Head Lighthouse fits perfectly into this scene of breathtaking beauty. Its brick tower is a solid piece of work, looking much today as it did a hundred years ago when construction crews built it—on the wrong cape. The lighthouse was meant for Cape Foulweather, about four miles to the north. The mistake doomed the nearby Yaquina Bay Light by making it unnecessary.

sailors could more easily reach assistance at the station. Ironically, two of the wrecks were namesakes—the *Yaquina City* and the *Yaquina Bay,* both lost on the nearby bar within a year of each other in 1887–88.

Completed in 1873, the lighthouse remains in astonishingly good condition, especially considering that little repair work has been done on the structure in more than a hundred years. Its masonry tower has conical walls ninety-three feet high, raising the focal plane of the light 162 feet above the sea. The lantern holds an extraordinary twelve-foot-high first-order Fresnel lens that casts a beam visible nineteen miles at sea. It is a fixed lens; the 1,000-watt globe inside flashes at intervals. To extend the reach of its warning, the station broadcasts a radio beacon.

Manufactured by the Barbier and Fenestre Company in Paris in 1868, the lens was shipped around stormy Cape Horn in a sailing schooner. Some parts of the lens inexplicably disappeared during the journey. Perhaps their loss was an omen of the confusing and unhappy events that were to follow. First, the lens and construction materials were landed in the wrong spot—Yaquina Head—rather than their intended destination—Cape Foulweather, several miles to the north. Then the landing itself did not go smoothly. More than one of the boats bringing supplies ashore overturned in the crashing surf, dumping their cargoes into the sea.

Luckily, the lens was not damaged, and its missing parts were soon replaced. But by the time the lens was assembled and shining from the top of the tower, it had become apparent to one and all that a lighthouse had not been needed here. Its beacon was redundant with that of the Yaquina Bay Lighthouse. Still, the new lighthouse was obviously superior to its neighbor. The first-order lens of its masonry tower far outshined the fifth-order lens of the wooden Yaquina Bay Lighthouse. So the fate of the older light was sealed and its light extinguished.

HOW TO GET THERE:

Located off Highway 101 about 4 miles north of Newport, the Yaquina Head Lighthouse is closed to the public except by special arrangement with the Yaquina Bay Coast Guard station at Newport. It can by seen from the highway, the government park, and the nearby beach.

As fog and foul weather roll in from the Pacific, the big Yaquina Head lens lights up to warn ships away from Oregon's rugged coast.

CAPE MEARES LIGHT

Tillamook, Oregon – 1890

Like the Yaquina Head Lighthouse well to the south, the old Cape Meares Lighthouse was misplaced by its builders. Government officials had planned to erect the lighthouse on Cape Lookout, but because of a mapmaker's error, it ended up instead at Cape Meares, about ten miles from its intended location. U.S. Coast Survey charts had reversed the names of the two capes. By the time the mistake was noticed late in 1889, the new lighthouse was already under construction.

The confusion and apparent waste of public money stirred considerable shouting and recrimination among bureaucrats and congressmen in Washington, D.C. But President Benjamin Harrison quieted the furor by placing his stamp of approval on the new site.

Completed in 1890, the octagonal iron tower was only thirty-eight feet tall and looked a bit like a squat chessboard rook. It stood on a towering cliff, however, which placed the light 217 feet above the breakers and made it one of the highest navigational aids in America. A huge Henry Lapaute first-order lens, illuminated by a coal-oil lamp, made the light visible from twenty-one miles at sea.

A veteran of three-quarters of a century of service to mariners, the old Cape Meares Lighthouse has been retired. In 1963 an unattractive concrete blockhouse took over its duties. While the new structure is hardly imposing, its 800,000-candlepower light is impressive. It can be seen from twenty-five miles at sea.

HOW TO GET THERE:

The Cape Meares Lighthouse is located in Cape Meares State Park, about 7 miles west of Highway 101 and Tillamook on Three Capes Loop Road. Visitors can park and walk down to the old lighthouse, inactive since 1963. The tower still houses the original first-order lens. Nearby is Cape Meares National Wildlife Refuge.

The older lighthouse is now a popular tourist attraction. Much to their discredit, vandals have damaged its magnificent lens on more than one occasion. The area around the lighthouse is now a state park and wildlife sanctuary.

Visitors enjoy a keeper's-eye view of the Pacific while inspecting the enormous, first-order Fresnel lens at the now-inactive Cape Meares Lighthouse. Its duties have been taken over by a nearby automated light.

LIGHTSHIP *COLUMBIA*

Astoria, Oregon – 1951

Among the last of America's lightships, the 128-foot-long *Columbia* was launched in Maine. For nearly three decades, beginning in 1951, she stood on station eight miles off the dangerous Columbia River bar. Retired in 1979, she has since been a prime attraction of the Columbia River Maritime Museum in Astoria.

HOW TO GET THERE:

Part of the Columbia River Maritime Museum, the Lightship *Columbia is moored on the Astoria waterfront at 1792 Marine Drive. Open daily until 5:00 P.M., the museum maintains the lightship as a historical attraction. For museum hours and tour information, call (503) 325–2323.*

Beached by a ferocious turn-of-the-century storm, an early Columbia River lightship is relaunched. Heavy chains and cables pull the ship toward the water. (Courtesy National Archives)

Where it was impossible or too costly to build coastal lighthouses, lightships guided mariners. Now on display in Astoria, the lightship Columbia *marked the treacherous Columbia River bar for more than thirty years.* (Courtesy John W. Weil)

CHAPTER TWO

Lights of
THE OLYMPIC COAST
WASHINGTON

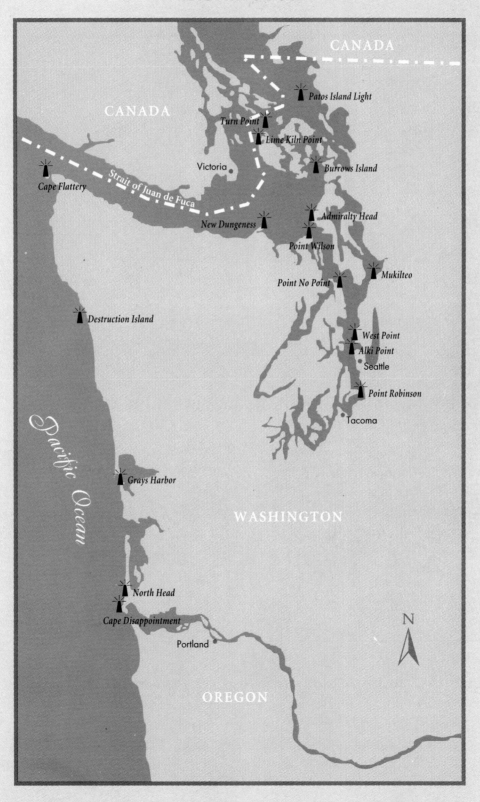

Although lighthouse keepers often faced loneliness and hardship, some perhaps considered their lives idyllic. Surrounded by lush summer growth, a 1940s-era keeper enjoys the company of his wife and family mutt at isolated Cape Flattery Light Station in Washington. (Courtesy U.S. Coast Guard)

ust as the northeastern corner of the United States is marked by a lighthouse—West Quoddy Light (see *New England Lighthouses*, The Globe Pequot Press, 1996)—so too is the northwestern corner (not counting Alaska). The Cape Flattery Light beams out into the Pacific from barren Tatoosh Island at the entrance of the Strait of Juan de Fuca. Thirty miles across the stormy strait is Canada's Vancouver Island.

Not only is Cape Flattery the most northwesterly lighthouse in the continental United States, it is also one of the nation's most isolated light stations. The sixty-five-foot stone tower and Cape Cod–style dwelling stand as a testament to the loneliness and hardiness of lighthouse keepers and their families.

Among the West's first great navigational sentinels, this lighthouse was completed and placed in operation in 1857, during the administration of President James Buchanan. The stone tower rose directly out of the keeper's dwelling so that he could climb its steps and service the light without braving harsh weather. Tatoosh Island is itself a hundred feet high so that the focal point of the light is 165 feet above the sea.

The original first-order Fresnel lens was manufactured in Paris in 1854. The lens had been purchased for the Point Loma Lighthouse in San Diego but was placed in the Cape Flattery Light instead because the former lighthouse was too small to hold a first-order lens. Its light still marks the cape. A red sector warns mariners of Duncan Rock, a ship-destroying rock that rises unexpectedly out of the turbulent Pacific waters.

A U.S. Signal Corps weather station was established on the island in 1883. Mother Nature gave the hardy weathermen plenty to measure—an average of 215 inches of rain a year and seasonal storms of prodigious ferocity.

KEEPERS, NOT HERMITS

Nowadays the Cape Flattery Lighthouse is automated. The mechanisms that control its light receive their instructions electronically, and Coast Guard operators and maintenance personnel need to visit the station only occasionally. But for more than a century, the light was operated manually by keepers who lived and worked at the station. Although their families often lived with them, theirs was a very lonely existence.

Today, of the hundreds of active lighthouses in the United States, only one—the Boston Harbor Lighthouse—has a keeper in residence. So, for all practical purposes, the profession of lighthouse keeper is extinct in America. But it is far from forgotten. Living at the very edge of the sea and maintaining their life-saving sentinels, the keepers and their lighthouses appeal to our romantic instincts.

It might logically be assumed that the keepers, because of their choice of profession, were hermits—lovers of craggy, storm-beaten rocks unpopulated except for birds, lichens, and themselves. Like most simplistic notions, however, this one is false. Generally speaking, people accepted work as lighthouse keepers, not because they were antisocial, but because it was a job. It offered them steady employment, certain if moderate pay, and a place to live.

Often, keepers and their families suffered greatly from their isolation, especially at remote stations such as Cape Flattery. Not long before the turn of the century, one Cape Flattery keeper found that he could no longer endure the loneliness of life on his faraway rock. Having decided to put an immediate end to his misery, he attempted suicide by jumping off one of the island's precipitous cliffs. The disconsolate keeper fell nearly a hundred feet onto the wave-swept boulders below, but some miracle preserved his life. Before the tide came up to swallow him, his assistants found him lying unconscious on the rocks. Hoisting him to safety, they carried him back to the keeper's dwelling. Later he was transferred to a hospital on the mainland where he recovered from his ordeals—both physical and psychological.

THE THUNDERBIRD ISLAND POTLATCH WAR

Vunerable to gales, blasted frequently by high winds, and under constant assault by the often freezing waters of the Pacific, remote Tatoosh Island could hardly be described as a paradise. Nonetheless, the Indians of Washington's Olympic Peninsula considered it something of a Valhalla. Braving the churning ocean in their dugout canoes, the Makah Indians gathered on Tatoosh—their word for "thunderbird," the native lightning god—to celebrate the summer and, occasionally, to bury their dead. Not surprisingly, they were reluctant to give the island up when officials in faraway Washington, D.C., selected it as an ideal location for a lighthouse.

When members of the West Coast Survey team came ashore on Tatoosh during the early 1850s, they found it occupied by a large band of Makahs who made them feel less than welcome. Fearing for their lives, the surveyors threw up a stockade and kept armed guards on alert at all times. The Indians were more curious than hostile, however—there was no attack. The Makahs had probably decided that the best defense against these intruders was to ignore them.

In 1853 a second survey team arrived on the island. They unintentionally brought with them a devastating weapon against which the Indians had no defense—smallpox. A raging epidemic killed more than 500 Makahs, over half the tribe. Understandably, the Indians blamed the strange foreign visitors, whom they referred to as "Bostons," for the horrible malady that had overtaken them. They called on neighboring tribes—even some that had been blood enemies—to help drive off the invaders. Soon, forty war canoes appeared off the island. Disguised as traders, the native warriors hoped to surprise their enemies and annihilate them. The surveyors saw through the ruse, however, and a few cannon shots from the survey steamer *Active* scattered the attackers.

Despite the attack and the prospect of future conflicts with the Makahs, the surveyors chose Tatoosh as a site for one of the first sixteen lighthouses to be built on the nation's Pacific seaboard. Construction got underway in the middle of 1855 and was completed eighteen months later, but not without plenty of trouble from the Indians. Resorting to a more passive form of harassment, the Makahs stole food, tools, building materials, and even clothing. Eternally curious, they got in the way of construction, and they kept workers in constant fear of being attacked. To hold the Indians at bay, the construction crews built a blockhouse and stocked it with plenty of muskets and gunpowder.

Even after the station went into operation in 1857, relations between the Makahs and lighthouse personnel continued to be strained. The first four keepers resigned their positions because, outnumbered hundreds to one by the local Indians, they naturally feared for their lives. Fortunately, they were wrong about the Makahs' hostile intentions. Given the odds, they would have lost their scalps at any time the Indians wished to take them. But they kept their hair, if not their jobs. The government replaced these reluctant employees with less timid keepers. Luckily for them and for the mariners who now depended on the Cape Flattery Light, their stand on the island did not prove their last.

The bad feelings between the Indians and whites on Tatoosh were to be expected, considering that the two radically different cultures were in collision here. Some of the discord might have been averted, however, had the white men taken time to study the customs of the Northwest Indians. The truth is, the Makahs felt the whites were not only unwanted intruders but quite ill mannered as well. The Indians measured a man's importance not by what he possessed but by how much he was willing to give away. Usually, the giving was done during a potlatch, a party at which the host showers gifts on his guests. The whites never held a potlatch for their new neighbors, so the Makahs thought them stingy, uncouth, and more or less worthless.

ISLAND *of* SORROWS

Although relations with the Makahs on Tatoosh were peaceful most of the time, white visitors had deadly encounters with Indians elsewhere along the Washington coast. In 1775 an expedition of Spanish explorers anchored its ships near where the Destruction Island Lighthouse now stands. A small boatload of seamen went ashore to forage for food and bring back fresh water. Instead they ran into a war party of Indians who made short work of them. In memory of their fallen shipmates, the Spanish named the place Isla de Dolores or Island of Sorrows.

Several years later a party of British foragers received the same fatal reception here. As a result, a nearby river and later the island as well were given the somber name "Destruction."

Sometimes the whites in the West were more endangered by their friends than by the Indians. While the Makahs at Cape Flattery never took up arms against the outnumbered keepers, two of the lighthouse men did try to shoot each other. During a breakfast argument, hot coffee was slung across the table and tempers flared. Scalded and red with anger, the two hotheads resolved to fight a duel to the death. In a field beside the light tower, they both emptied their pistols without scoring a hit. By this time heads had cooled, and the gunmen decided that it was possible, after all, for the two of them to live on the island in peace. Only much later did they learn that a friend had loaded their pistols with blanks.

Besieged by ocean, Cape Flattery Light marks the Strait of Juan de Fuca. (Photo by Bob and Sandra Shanklin)

CAPE DISAPPOINTMENT LIGHT

Ilwaco, Washington – 1856

It was near midnight—the middle of a workday at a lighthouse. Soaked by rain and sea spray and buffeted by high winds, a young third assistant keeper clung to a lightning-rod cable. Lowering himself down the slick side of the fifty-three-foot conical masonry tower, he tried deperately to gain reentry.

George Esterbrook, seventeen years old at the time, had stepped onto the tower's catwalk to wipe frost from the lantern panes, when the wind blew the access door shut. Try as he might, he could not get it open.

Hanging from the cable, he lowered himself over the edge and, dangling more than fifty feet above the ground, swung himself onto a secondary catwalk below the lantern. Momentarily stunned by the fall, he shook his head and found an unlatched door. Once he was safely inside, the exhaustion of his ordeal caught up with him. He lay in a heap on the watch-room floor until it came time to rewind the light's weight mechanism. Then he went back to work.

Esterbrook later became a physician. It is said he

Many vessels have met destruction on or near this stony cape that bears the name "Disappointment." Poised on top of the cliff, the Cape Disappointment Lighthouse warns mariners of danger. To the right, the Columbia River flows into the Pacific. (Courtesy U.S. Coast Guard)

applied the same dedication to the medical profession that he had to being an assistant lighthouse keeper.

Cape Disappointment is a bold headland overlooking the meeting place of the Columbia River and the Pacific Ocean. It was named by fur trader John Meares, who mistook the headland for another landfall and, realizing his error, sailed away in disappointment.

The captains of many other ships have encountered another, more bitter, form of disappointment at the cape. Countless vessels have foundered here. The Columbia is America's second largest river. It churns the ocean near its entrance, and its bar is particularly treacherous.

The U.S. Coast Survey recommended erecting a lighthouse on the cape as early as 1848, but eight years went by before one was finally built. The oil lamp inside its first-order Fresnel lens was first lit on October 15, 1856, the same year that James Buchanan was elected president of the United States. Construction of the Cape Disappointment Lighthouse proved extraordinarily expensive. It cost $38,500, more than a quarter of the $148,000 appropriation set aside by Congress for the construction of the first nine Pacific Coast lighthouses.

Before the lighthouse marked the cape, settlers had used a white flag in the day and set trees on fire at night to guide mariners. Later they created a day mark by cutting off the tops of trees growing on the headland. Meanwhile, the flow of vessels in and out of the river increased steadily. Most were engaged in hauling lumber or involved in the fur trade with China.

Completion of the Cape Disappointment lighthouse was delayed by an incident that dramatized its necessity. In the fall of 1853 the bark *Oriole* foundered on the Columbia River bar while attempting to deliver building materials for the tower. No lives were lost, but construction of the tower had to await another shipment. Meanwhile, workers built a trail to the summit of the cape, cleared a site, and prepared ground for a foundation. The notorious raininess of the Northwest hampered construction. Much of the work was done in downpours and in deep mud.

The lighthouse was designed to minimize damage by moisture. Of particular concern was the station's oil lamp, which was brought around Cape Horn in a sailing ship. The lamp had five wicks arranged in a circle with an eighteen-inch diameter, and it consumed 170 gallons of whale oil per month. With each gallon of oil burned, it produced a quart of water vapor. Grooves were placed in the tower's window frames to allow drainage, and eagle-headed gargoyles were placed beneath the roof overhang to drain water that condensed on the ceiling.

A 1,600-pound bronze bell was installed as a fog signal. Unfortunately, dead spots and roaring surf often made the bell impossible to hear, and so it was disconnected. The problem of aiding mariners caught in the fog was not solved until well into the twentieth century, when a radio beacon was installed.

Although the light and bell saved many ships from destruction, other vessels were not so fortunate. To reduce the loss of lives in wrecks, keeper Joel Munson, who served at Cape Disappointment from 1865 to 1877, organized a volunteer lifesaving crew. Later the government established a permanent lifesaving station at Fort Canby, whose guns surrounded the lighthouse. (Built in 1864, the fort was a troublesome neighbor. The concussion of its cannons fired in practice often shattered windows and even destroyed the station's original fog-bell house.) The fort's lifesaving team was called into action by the firing of a small cannon near the tower. In 1884 the Fort Canby Lifesavers rescued 175 passengers from the liner *Queen of the Pacific* after she ran aground near Clatsop Beach, Oregon. (The liner was later refloated and returned to service.) Today the Coast Guard Station at Cape Disappointment monitors sea traffic with a battery of sophisticated electronic instruments and continues to rescue mariners in distress.

The Cape Disappointment Light is one of the oldest standing structures in the Pacific Northwest and is the oldest lighthouse in Washington.

HOW TO GET THERE:

From Ilwaco follow signs for Cape Disappointment and Fort Canby State Park. The park is open throughout the year during daylight hours. Markers inside the park direct visitors to the lighthouse. A close-up look requires a brief hike from the parking area. Tours are available on Fridays during the summer. For information on tours call the Lewis and Clark Interpretive Center at (206) 642–3029. The center itself, well worth a visit, is open daily, 9:00 a.m.–5:00 P.M. from May through September and on weekends from October through April.

NORTH HEAD LIGHT

Ilwaco, Washington – 1898

For the keeper of the North Head Lighthouse, World War II came very close to home. One night not long after the Japanese surprise attack on Pearl Harbor, an enemy submarine surfaced and opened fire on Fort Stevens, located on the opposite (Oregon) side of the Columbia River. Hearing the boom of the submarine's deck gun, the keeper shut off the light. Likely he stood in the darkened lantern room atop the light tower and watched the bright flashes of the gun and its exploding shells. The raid was brief, and the Japanese did not return.

The North Head Light has seen a lot of excitement since it was completed in 1898. Built at a cost of $25,000,

the station was established to warn ships approaching the Columbia from the north. Mariners complained that they could not see the nearby Cape Disappointment Light from that direction. By the time the new lighthouse was built, the headland's beaches had already taken an impressive toll of ships.

As their vessel plowed through a heavy fog in 1882, the crew of *Harvest Home*, bound for Port Townsend, heard roosters crowing in a nearby barn. That's the only warning they got before the *Harvest Home* slammed into the shore. At low tide the fortunate crewmen were able to walk to safety. Local residents helped salvage most of the

The impressive North Head Lighthouse guards one of the country's windiest locations. Winds on this peninsula have attained speeds of 150 miles per hour. (Photo by John W. Weil)

cargo of wagons, but the vessel itself was a total loss and was left to rot. The following year the bark *Whistler* suffered a similar fate. Four years later so did the barkentine *Grace Roberts*.

During a fierce gale in 1891, the British ship *Strath-blane* ran aground on the sandy peninsula just before daylight. The crew despaired as the vessel began to break up. To save them, the Fort Canby Lifesaving Service team swung into action. With keeper Al Harris in charge, the station crewmen loaded their boats onto a narrow-gauge train and sped to the scene of the wreck.

By midmorning the lifesavers were pushing one of the boats into the heavy surf. Twice the boat was swamped, and finally it overturned. Afraid the boat might never reach them, sailors on the foundering *Strathbland* started jumping overboard to swim ashore. Twenty-four were saved by the lifesaving crew. Two others were pulled to safety by quick-thinking local residents who galloped into the surf on their horses. The struggling sailors grabbed the horses' tails and were dragged out of the sea, alive though a bit humiliated.

The white tower of the North Head Lighthouse is sixty-five feet tall and stands on the edge of a cliff almost 130 feet high. Originally, it was fitted with a first-order Fresnel lens taken from the nearby Cape Disappointment Lighthouse, which in turn received a fourth-order lens. During the 1930s the big, veteran lens was put on display in the cape's interpretive center and again was replaced with a much smaller fourth-order lens.

North Head is said to be the third windiest spot in the nation. Winds blast across the peninsula at speeds clocked at up to 150 miles per hour. Trees, chimneys, and fences have been flattened by these gale-force winds. In 1932 a wild duck blown off course and out of control by the wind slammed into the lantern, shattering a window and even chipping prisms in the lens. With the wind in mind, builders fixed handrails to the lantern-room window frames so the keepers could grasp them firmly while cleaning the glass. Legend has it that a keeper's wife, unable to bear the howling of the winds, jumped to her death from the cliff.

Until the light was automated in 1961, keepers entered the tower through a small workroom that was edged in mosaic tile. Today this practical but handsome room still has its original desk and wood-burning stove. The station's two dwellings are now occupied by Fort Canby State Park personnel. When

accompanied by guides, visitors are allowed to climb the sixty-nine steps to the top of the tower. The enormous lens that once crowned the tower is a prime attraction at the Lewis and Clark Interpretive Center at Fort Canby State Park.

The tower of the North Head Lighthouse looms above a marker showing its precise latitude and longitude.

HOW TO GET THERE:

From the town of Ilwaco off Highway 101, follow signs to Cape Disappointment and Fort Canby State Park. Markers inside the park point the way to the lighthouse. The nearby Lewis and Clark Interpretive Center is well worth a visit. It is open daily (including holidays) from 10:00 A.M. to 5:00 P.M. Fort Canby is open all year long during daylight hours.

GRAYS HARBOR LIGHT

Westport, Washington – 1898

Towering more than one hundred feet from its base to its lantern, the octagonal Grays Harbor Lighthouse is one of the tallest on the Pacific coast. With its white masonry tower and black lantern, the nearly century-old structure is an architectural masterpiece, a fact not lost on the thousands of photographers who flock here to capture the graceful lighthouse on film.

Situated about midway along the Pacific coast of Washington State, the lighthouse serves the harbor and the fishing town of Westport. It also serves as a coastal light, guiding ships through a dark stretch between Willapa Bay to the south and the Destruction Island Light to the north.

The third-order Fresnel lens at the top of the tower was made in Paris by the Henry Lapaute Company. It has three bull's-eyes about eight inches in diameter, emitting white and red flashes. The white sector is visible from twenty-three miles away.

Established in 1898, the station was provided with a steam-powered fog siren housed in a separate building. In fog or heavy weather the keeper stoked the boiler's fires. The station now has a diaphone, or two-tone, fog signal as well as a powerful radio beacon.

At least fifty ships have met their end near the entrance to Grays Harbor, an area frequently racked by savage squalls. No one is sure how many fishing boats and other small craft have been fatally trapped here by storms or by the confusion of sandy shallows. Sailors caught in a storm see the Grays Harbor beacon as a signpost pointing the way to safer waters.

HOW TO GET THERE:

The lighthouse is open very limited hours on summer holiday weekends. It can, however, be viewed anytime from Ocean Avenue in the delightful seaside town of Westport. For information on visits call the Westport Coast Guard Station at (206) 268–0121.

Crowned by its glowing lantern room, the octagonal masonry tower of the Grays Harbor Lighthouse stands like an empress above a forest of conifers.

DESTRUCTION ISLAND LIGHT

Destruction Island, Washington – 1891

Destruction Island was considered a dismal and unlucky place by European mariners who first set foot on its beaches during the 1700s—and with good reason. Two Spanish ships anchored off the island in 1775 and sent sailors ashore to fill casks with water. The unsuspecting shore party was set upon and slaughtered by Indians. As a memorial to their lost crewmen, the Spaniards named the place Isla de Delores or Island of Sorrows. A few years later the crew of a British vessel had a similar tragic experience here and afterwards called the unhappy landfall Destruction Island.

The name proved an apt one, as the rocky island would exact a heavy toll on vessels and sailors braving the waters off the Washington coast. The island represented such a threat to shipping that it was selected as the site for one of the first lighthouses on the U.S. West Coast. In 1855 Congress appropriated $45,000 for the project, but even this considerable sum—a fortune at the time—proved woefully inadequate. The Destruction Island station would not be completed and in service for more than three decades.

Spurred on by a sharp increase in shipping along the Washington coast and the lengthening list of wrecks off the island, work on the lighthouse resumed in 1888. To build the tower, dwelling, and other structures, materials had to be lightered ashore from a tender anchored in a nearby cove. Building and fitting out the isolated lighthouse took more than three years. The steam-driven fog signal went into service in November 1891, and one month later the lamps were lit in the tower.

In recognition of the station's importance and the considerable threat of this rugged coast to shipping, the Destruction Island Lighthouse was given a first-order Fresnel lens. The huge French-made lens has 1,176 separate, hand-polished prisms and is one of the last of its kind still in use today.

Until 1989 the isolated station was maintained by a full-time resident staff. Station personnel remained on duty for six weeks at a stretch and then received two weeks of shore leave. Mail and supplies arrived by tender every few weeks. Since 1989 the lighthouse has been automated, with maintenance crews paying brief visits every few months.

HOW TO GET THERE:

Destruction Island Light is off limits to the public but can be seen from a parking area along Highway 101 about a mile south of Ruby Beach.

(Courtesy U.S. Coast Guard)

NEW DUNGENESS LIGHT

Dungeness, Washington – 1857

The lighthouse that stands today near the tip of the eight-mile-long Dungeness Spit is the same one built there in 1857, more than 135 years ago. Nowadays, however, the tower is only about half as tall as it once was. Suffering from age and structural weakness, the original hundred-foot tower was in danger of collapsing by the 1920s. Engineers decided the structural problems could be solved by lopping off the top thirty-seven feet of the tower, and that is what was done.

The original tower sported a very unusual color scheme. The top half of the brick tower was painted black, while the bottom was painted white. This arrangement made the tower seem top-heavy when viewed from a distance and no doubt caused more than one sailor to rub his eyes and shake his head before taking a second look. For good measure, the lantern was painted red. When the lighthouse was renovated in 1927, it was given a much more conventional paint job—white from top to bottom.

During its early years the light guided not only ships and fishing vessels but also canoes paddled by Indian warriors prepared to do battle on Dungeness Spit. Traditionally, tribes on opposite sides of the Strait of Juan de Fuca had used the spit as a convenient battleground for settling differences. After the lighthouse was built, they continued the practice, but now the place was easier to find. Apparently happy to have a light to guide them to their dark and bloody work, they never molested the keepers—only one another.

The lighthouse and the spit on which it stands took their name from Dungeness Point in England, coincidently famed for *its* magnificent lighthouse. Like its British namesake, Dungeness Spit is a ship killer. The list of the vessels wrecked on its sands is nearly endless. Mariners have long referred to it as "Shipwreck Spit."

HOW TO GET THERE:

New Dungeness Lighthouse is accessible only by boat or by means of an 8-mile hike along highly scenic Dungeness Spit, a protected wildlife area. Take Highway 101 west of Sequim and then turn north, following signs to the wildlife area. The lighthouse can be seen from a distance by taking the Sequim Scenic Loop Road. For information on tours call the Coast Guard at (206) 457–4401.

New Dungeness Lighthouse, shown here as it looked in 1898. (Courtesy National Archives)

POINT WILSON LIGHT

Port Townsend, Washington – 1914

It was a sickening sound—the grinding and screeching of one metal ship's hull against another. It is easy to imagine that lighthouse keeper William Thomas winced when he heard it on April 1, 1921. Point Wilson was cloaked that day in a blanket of fog, thick even by Northwest standards, so Thomas had no trouble guessing what had happened: Two vessels lost in the fog slammed into each other. Thomas immediately set to work organizing a rescue effort.

The rescuers soon discovered a tragedy in the making. The freighter *West Hartland* had collided with the *Governor*, a crowded passenger liner. The *Governor* sank quickly

At dusk a Fresnel lens outshines the last pink rays of sunlight brightening the walls of Point Wilson Lighthouse in Washington.

in 600 feet of water, but fast work by rescuers and the liner's crew made an orderly abandonment possible. In all, eight lives were lost, but hundreds might have drowned. The *West Hartland,* her bow stove in all the way to the Number One hatch, was towed to a Seattle dry dock.

At about the time of the *Governor/West Hartland* accident, the last of the West Coast merchant sailing fleet was being destroyed by another sort of accident—a collision with history. The destruction had begun decades earlier, as one by one, steel-hulled and steam-powered freighters replaced the old sailing schooners. The lighthouse at Point Wilson is symbolic of this shift.

Traditionally, sailing ships had approached Port Townsend, Washington, along the eastern shore of Admiralty Inlet. A light established in 1861 on Whidbey Island guided them into port. But steam-powered vessels, with their deeper drafts, favored the inlet's western side. As sail gave way to steam, shippers and citizens of Port Townsend, who hoped to make their city the state's foremost port, lobbied to get a light on the western shore, where traffic was steadily increasing. Eventually, the Lighthouse Board responded and erected a white frame tower on Point Wilson.

On the evening of December 15, 1879, keeper David Littlefield lit the tower's oil lamp for the first time. A fourth-order Fresnel lens focused the light, visible from any point along a sweeping 270 degrees of horizon. Soon, a fog signal was placed in an adjacent building. A twelve-inch steam whistle, it was powered by a wood-burning boiler.

Exactly one year to the day after the station's lamp first burned, the American bark *David Hoadley* ran aground on a beach not far from the lighthouse. A flooding tide lifted the *Hoadley's* wooden hull far up on the beach so that, when the tide receded, the bark was left high and dry. The crew was able to climb over the side and walk ashore, barely getting their feet wet. Salvage efforts failed, and the *Hoadley* became a rotting hulk.

A Civil War veteran who had arrived in Port Townsend in 1867, Littlefield served as keeper for only a few years. Having married Maria Hastings, a local woman of some social standing, Littlefield became a prominent figure in the town, eventually serving as its mayor.

By 1904 high tides such as the one that had doomed the *Hoadley* had eroded much of the beach in front of the lighthouse and soon threatened the tower itself. To save the lighthouse 1,500 tons of rock and rubble were piled up to the east and west of the tower, but even stone could not hold back the sea forever.

A new lighthouse was commissioned and was ready for service by 1914. Constructed of reinforced concrete, the forty-six-foot octagonal tower was designed to reduce wind pressure on the building. Now automated, Point Wilson Light is monitored by computer from the Coast Guard Air Station at Port Angeles.

HOW TO GET THERE:

The Point Wilson Lighthouse is located in Fort Worden State Park at the far northeastern corner of the Olympic Peninsula. Take Route 20 to Port Townsend and then follow signs to the park, which is open all year during daylight hours. The lighthouse is open for tours only by special arrangement with the Coast Guard. For information call (206) 457–4401.

POINT NO POINT LIGHT

Hansville, Washington – 1880

The pilots of ships moving up from Puget Sound into Admiralty Inlet often notice a prominent headland sweeping up from the southwest. They may think they are seeing Foulweather Bluff at the far end of Washington's long central peninsula, but they are mistaken. This land feature is the appropriately named Point No Point.

A key navigational light has shone from Point No Point since 1880. Built on a forty-acre tract acquired by the Lighthouse Service for just $1,800, the Point No Point Light Station is a near twin of its sister lighthouse on West Point near Seattle. Both stations consist of a rectangular fog-signal building with a squat tower barely peeking through its roof and a separate keeper's dwelling. The lanterns of both towers originally held bull's-eye-type fourth-order Fresnel lenses. These lenses focused the light into a series of flashes that could be seen from about fifteen miles away.

John Maggs, Point No Point's first keeper, had a family, and a baby girl was born at the station just three months after its flashing light went into operation. A

schooner brought a cow from the mainland to provide milk for the child.

Maggs's relations with his first assistant, a man named Manning, were not peaceful. After a disagreement over the operation of the fog bell, knives and pistols were brandished. Luckily, no one was injured, and the unruly assistant was soon replaced.

Over the years, the Point No Point Lighthouse saved many ships from disaster. One that it could not save was the small passenger liner *Admiral Sampson*, which sank off the point in 1914 after colliding with a second liner, the *Princess Victoria*. Eleven passengers and crew went down with the *Sampson*, including Captain Zimro Moore.

HOW TO GET THERE:

From Port Gamble follow Highway 104 South and then Highway 305 East. Then turn north onto Hansville Road Northeast and follow it for approximately 10 miles to the town of Hansville. Signs there point the way to the lighthouse.

(Photo by Bob and Sandra Shanklin)

POINT ROBINSON LIGHT

Tacoma, Washington – 1887 and 1915

Pilots of vessels plying the Puget Sound waters between Seattle and Tacoma keep a sharp eye out for the Point Robinson Light. Located on the eastern end of Maury Island, the light marks a key safe channel in this narrow but heavily trafficked waterway.

A fog signal was placed on the point in 1885 to protect ships from running aground on the island. Particularly threatening was a low, sandy spit extending several hundred yards out into Puget Sound. Lighthouse officials soon concluded that the fog signal alone was inadequate, and in 1887 a modest lantern and lens were added to the station.

As shipping increased in the lower Puget Sound, the station's importance grew. In 1915 a full-fledged lighthouse was established here. It consisted of a pair of keeper's dwellings and a thirty-eight-foot concrete tower and lantern room containing a fifth-order Fresnel lens. The cylindrical tower and fog-signal building stand approximately 150 yards out on the spit.

With its peaceful, scenic location and proximity to Tacoma and Seattle, Robinson Point Lighthouse was once a very popular duty station for keepers and their families. Nowadays the light is automated and continues to do its job without the help of resident keepers.

HOW TO GET THERE:

The lighthouse is located on the northeast corner of Maury Island, just across from the larger and more populous Vashon Island in Puget Sound. The station is open to the public from noon until 4:00 P.M. on weekends. For information on tours and transportation, call (206) 463–2951.

Point Robinson Lighthouse guides vessels through the key Seattle-to-Tacoma passage in heavily traveled Puget Sound. Located on Maury Island on the west side of the main shipping channel, the 38-foot octagonal masonry tower and attached fog-signal building were built in 1915.

ALKI POINT LIGHT

Seattle, Washington – 1887 and 1913

hrusting far out into the blue waters of Puget Sound, wedge-shaped Alki Point makes a notable impression on mariners, who must swing their ships wide to avoid it. When he anchored his sloop of war *Discovery* near here in 1792, British Captain George Vancouver recognized the strategic nature of the point, noting that it marked the southern entrance to Elliot's Bay. Later, American explorer Charles Wilkes visited the point and thought it a likely spot for a fortress. Federal surveyors who charted the entire West Coast during 1855–56 apparently agreed and gave it the it name "Battery Point."

Perhaps hoping it would develop into a burgeoning commercial center, early settlers called the point "New York," but it was destined to become neither a West Coast Manhattan nor a military outpost. Overshadowed by bustling Seattle only a few miles to the northeast, the point languished, almost completely ignored by commercial interests and government officials. Disappointed landowners scrapped earlier names and took to calling it "Alki Point" after a Chinook Indian word meaning "by-and-by" or "all in good time."

Alki Point was of obvious importance to shipping both as a daymark showing the way to Seattle and a threat in fog and at night. Even so, no light was displayed here until the 1880s, when landowner Hans Martin Hanson hung up a small lantern as a humanitarian gesture. In 1887 the U.S. Lighthouse Service improved the light, installing a small lantern and lens. Hanson was paid $15 per month to keep the lamp burning.

With shipping traffic between Seattle and Tacoma to the south on the increase, the government decided in 1913 to build a full-fledged lighthouse on Alki Point. Buying land from Manson's heirs for $10,000, the service built an octagonal, thirty-seven-foot-tall masonry tower, attached fog-signal building, and nearby keeper's dwelling. The station employed a fourth-order Fresnel lens and diesel-compressor–driven fog trumpets. Originally, a brass kerosene lamp generated the light, but in 1918 an electric bulb system was installed. Although automated in 1970, the light remains in operation, flashing white every two seconds.

HOW TO GET THERE:

lki Point Light is located just to the south of the public beach at Alki. To reach the beach and lighthouse from Seattle, follow I-5 South, then the West Seattle Freeway to the Harbor Avenue exit. Turn right on Harbor Avenue and follow it (Harbor Avenue eventually becomes Beach Drive) along the water to the lighthouse. An active Coast Guard facility, the lighthouse is not regularly open to the public.

WEST POINT LIGHT

Seattle, Washington – 1881

Rising twenty-three feet above a low sandy point at the north entrance to Elliott Bay, West Point Lighthouse has welcomed ships to Seattle for more than a hundred years. Situated five miles from the city's thriving urban business core, the old lighthouse stands at the foot of Magnolia Bluff in Seattle's Discovery Park.

The little lighthouse was built in 1881 at a cost to taxpayers of $25,000, a rather princely sum in those days. It was originally fitted with a complex fourth-order Fresnel lens. Manufactured by a veteran lensmaker in Paris, it had twelve bull's-eyes to focus its light and cause it to flash. The light first shined on November 15, 1881, and, according to a Coast Guard estimate, has since put in more than 400,000 hours of nighttime service. Its white beam is visible from fifteen miles away.

The station has employed a variety of fog signals, the first of them a bell placed in the tower. Later the station warned ships with a steam whistle and, later still, a Daboll fog signal (named for its inventor), which directed a whistle blast through a large trumpetlike device.

Earlier in this century the lighthouse was a favorite duty station for career coastguardsman Christian Fritz. The gentle landscape allowed Mrs. Fritz, who was blind, to roam freely on the premises with her Boxer guide dog Cookie. The faithful Boxer clung to the side of his mistress as she cleaned the house or sat weaving, a favorite hobby.

Tiny West Point Lighthouse, located in Seattle's Discovery Park, was among the last lights in the West to be automated. It had a resident keeper until 1985. (Courtesy U.S. Coast Guard)

While Fritz, a chief boatswain's mate, tended to the light, Mrs. Fritz, Cookie, and the Fritzes' daughter Christy would take long strolls. Unlike the terrain surrounding most lighthouses, there were no precipices here to endanger them.

Fritz was not the only coastguardsman who considered West Point an idyllic station. When the lighthouse has its one hundredth birthday in 1981, keeper Marvin Gerber climbed onto the roof and poured champagne over it. Ironically, Gerber was to be among the light's last keepers. It was automated in 1985.

One of the first keepers was George Fonda, who came to the station in 1883. Fonda became an apparently unwilling model for the Lighthouse Service when it tried out a new uniform on him. Consisting of navy blue trousers, a matching double-breasted coat with brass buttons, and a billed cap, the uniform was intended to raise the esteem of the lighthouse keepers and foster esprit de corps. But for Fonda, wearing the new uniform was a chore. It is said he wore it only when he knew inspectors or important guests were arriving. He must have grumbled and donned the fancy uniform frequently, because the station's guest registry is long and impressive.

People continue to visit the light to this day, but there is no longer a keeper to welcome them. Nonetheless, visitors will find much that is worth seeing. Most of the station's original equipment is on display in the original buildings. Just north of the lighthouse is the Lake Washington Ship Canal and the Hiram M. Chittenden Locks, which link Puget Sound to lakes Union and Washington.

HOW TO GET THERE:

A popular attraction of Seattle's Discovery Park, the lighthouse is located about 1½ miles from the entrance. Most visitors choose to take the convenient park shuttle bus to the lighthouse grounds. Those who wish to drive should get a parking permit at park headquarters. A pleasant way to enjoy an exterior view of the lighthouse is to take a relaxed stroll along West Point Beach. The park visitors' center is open daily until 5:00 P.M. but is closed on holidays. Park roads are closed to vehicles after 11:00 P.M. each night.

MUKILTEO LIGHT

Mukilteo, Washington – 1906

The Mukilteo Lighthouse stands on historic ground. Isaac Stevens, governor of the Washington Territory, signed a treaty here with the northwestern Indians in 1855. The name is an English version of a native American word meaning "good place for camping," and indeed Indians often gathered on this point of land in the days before whites took the land for their own.

Early in this century the Lighthouse Board decided to place a light and fog signal on the point to help guide vessels headed for Everett. Completed in 1906, the Victorian-style structure was fitted with a fourth-order Fresnel lens and equipped with a Daboll trumpet to warn ships plowing blindly through fog or heavy weather.

According to visitors, the station's dwelling was quite comfortable and was warmed by steam heat. The first keeper was Peter Christianson, who must have felt very much at home there. He remained on the job until 1925, when he died at the lighthouse of natural causes.

In 1960 the Coast Guard planned to replace the station's Fresnel lens with an airport-type beacon. Residents of Mukilteo and other nearby towns protested, however, and the old Fresnel remains in operation to this day, sending out a flash of white light every five second.

HOW TO GET THERE:

Active since 1906, the Mukilteo Lighthouse contains a Coast Guard photographic exhibit on the lighthouses of Puget Sound. Located in Mukilteo near the landing for the Whidbey Island ferry, the wood-frame structure is open to the public during the afternoon on weekends. For exact hours and other information, call (206) 355–2611.

The Mukilteo Lighthouse overlooks Possession Sound in Washington State. The thirty-foot octagonal tower is attached to the fog-signal building.

ADMIRALTY HEAD LIGHT

Whidbey Island, Washington – 1903

Built during the months just prior to the Civil War, the ancestor of the Admiralty Head Lighthouse was among the first lighthouses in the West. The frame structure was begun in August 1860 and completed late the following January, only weeks before the guns began to roar at Fort Sumter on the other side of the continent.

Located atop a knob called Red Bluff, the tower rose forty-one feet from base to lantern and had a fourth-order Fresnel lens. The station's fixed white light could be seen from about sixteen miles and welcomed Puget Sound marine traffic into Admiralty Inlet.

William Robertson, a Democrat, was hired as keeper during the last months of the James Buchanan adminis-

Used by the U.S. Army as an officer's residence, the Admiralty Head Lighthouse was abandoned after World War II. Its walls badly discolored in this photograph taken during the 1950s, the old lighthouse looks ready for a wrecking crane. Actually, it was about to receive a fresh coat of paint and begin a new life as a historic attraction. (Courtesy Washington State Parks and Recreation Commission)

tration. But as soon as Republican Abraham Lincoln had settled into the White House, Robertson found himself without a job.

During the Spanish-American War era, the army decided to build a fort on Red Bluff to protect the entrance to the inlet. To make room for guns and soldiers at newly established Fort Casey, the lighthouse was demolished. A replacement house, built on Admiralty Head, was ready for duty by 1903.

The brick tower rose only a few feet higher than the attached two-story residence. But the elevation of Admiralty Head placed the focal plane 127 feet above sea level. Focused by the station's original lens, the light could be seen from seventeen miles out into the sound.

The Admiralty Head Lighthouse had an even shorter active life than its predecessor, however. Changes in channels and shipping routes made the station obsolete, and it was discontinued in 1927. Soon the lantern was removed and placed atop the newly renovated New Dungeness Lighthouse. During World War II the lighthouse served as quarters for an officer at the nearby fort. Today the restored lighthouse is a museum and popular tourist attraction.

HOW TO GET THERE:

The lighthouse is located in Fort Casey State Park near the Keystone–Port Townsend slip, a few miles from the historic town of Coupeville on Whidbey Island. The park is open all year during daylight hours, but visitors may tour the lighthouse only during the summer.

The Admiralty Head Lighthouse served ships entering Puget Sound until the 1920s, when it was discontinued.

The pristine, forested setting of the Burrows Island Lighthouse adds extra attraction to this lovely old light station. Built in 1906, its thirty-four-foot frame tower and attached fog-signal building have served well for more than ninety years. A rambling two-story keeper's dwelling stands at the edge of the woods. A nearby landing and boom were once used to bring ashore supplies delivered by Coast Guard tenders. (Photo by Bob and Sandra Shanklin)

LIGHTS OF THE SAN JUAN ISLANDS

Turn Point Light – 1893
Patos Island Light – 1908
Lime Kiln Light – 1914

San Juan Islands, Washington

Pleasure boaters, yachtsmen, and ferry pilots who frequent the San Juans, an unspoiled chain of 172 islands in the straits between Washington State and Canada, know that navigation here can be difficult and dangerous. A tangle of narrow passages separate the islands, some of which are large enough for several towns and harbors, while others are no more than a scrape of exposed rock. Three major lighthouses mark the way for

mariners. Built in 1893, Turn Point Lighthouse shines from a squat, sixteen-foot concrete tower on the northwest end of Stuart Island. The thirty-eight-foot wooden tower of Patos Island Lighthouse, completed in 1908, stands on the western side of a scenic, 260-acre islet in the northern part of the chain. The octagonal tower of Lime Kiln Lighthouse dates from 1920 and marks the key shipping channel through Haro Strait.

Turn Point Lighthouse guards the rocky shores of Stuart Island in the idyllic San Juans, frequented in summer by yachts. The lens is located on a concrete pillar in front of the old keeper's dwelling and fog-signal building, which date to 1893. (Photo by Bob and Sandra Shanklin)

The Patos Island Lighthouse, now automated, helps boaters navigate the tangle of narrow passages separating the 172 islands and islets in the San Juan chain. Patos Island is a favorite haunt of picnickers. (Photo by Bob and Sandra Shanklin)

Lime Kiln Lighthouse faces the main shipping channel to the west of San Juan Island. At night dozens of navigation lights can be seen from this point. (Photo by Bob and Sandra Shanklin)

Completed in 1860, historic Fisgard Lighthouse, near Victoria, stands proudly among Canada's famed "Imperial Lights."
Funded by Britain's Board of Trade, it was built with bricks and fittings imported from England. Fisgard's first keeper was also
an import, an English lighthouse handyman named George Davies.

HOW TO GET THERE:

Access to the San Juan Islands and their light-houses is by boat or ferry. For information and schedules, contact the Washington State Ferry Service at (206) 464–6400.

CHAPTER THREE

Lights of
THE CANADIAN PACIFIC
BRITISH COLUMBIA

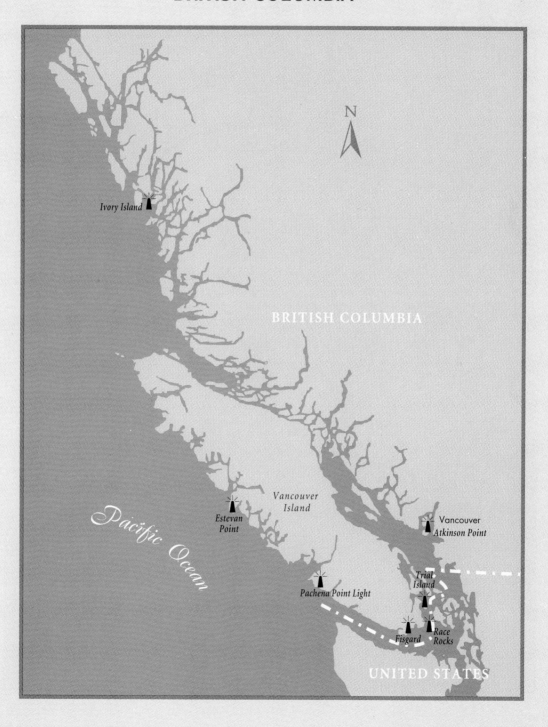

N

BRITISH COLUMBIA

Ivory Island

Pacific Ocean

Vancouver Island

Estevan Point

Vancouver
Atkinson Point

Pachena Point Light

Trial Island

Fisgard *Race Rocks*

UNITED STATES

The Pachena Point Lighthouse on Vancouver Island's rugged outer coast stands near the spot where the Valencia wrecked in 1906 with a loss of 117 lives. The lighthouse, with it rotating Fresnel lens, entered service in 1908. (Photo by Michael Mitchell)

ad the powerful beacon of the Pachena Point Lighthouse been shining on the night of January 22, 1906, the destruction of the *Valencia* (described on pages 2–6) might have been avoided. Unfortunately, for the *Valencia* and the 117 passengers and crew who perished in her wreck, the Pachena Point station had not yet been funded. There was no light to warn them away from the deadly rocks off the point.

A LIGHT on the POINT

Spurred by the *Valencia* tragedy, Canadian maritime officials commissioned a lighthouse for Pachena Point, and within months after the sinking, construction was under way. As with many lighthouses along the wild and rugged British Columbian coast, building a tower and dwelling on the isolated point required Herculean efforts. With only precarious road links to Victoria and Nanaimo, most materials and supplies had to be brought in by ship. Delayed by storms and driving rains that often lasted for weeks, the work dragged on month after month. What is worse, the heavy rains were undermining the construction site. In February 1908 a landslide carried away the partially built tower along with a large quantity of supplies, and the construction crew had to start all over again.

Eventually the lighthouse was completed, however, and during the late spring of 1908, workers were able to install the station's enormous first-order Fresnel lens atop the wooden tower. Together with machinery that rotated the big lens, the lantern assembly weighed more than thirty-eight tons.

On the evening of May 21, the lamps were lit and the lens's giant bull's-eyes threw out their first powerful flashes. Sailors were able to see the four-million-candlepower beacon from more than thirty-five miles away.

Over the years the Pachena Point Light has, no doubt, saved many ships and mariners from a tragic end. Unfortunately, John Richardson, the station's first keeper, would not be spared a tragedy of his own. Richardson was a bachelor, and during his first months of duty at the point, his sister Gertrude served with him as an assistant. Apparently overwhelmed by the isolation of Pachena Point, Gertrude Richardson began to hallucinate, and one day in the autumn of 1908 jumped to her death from the cliffs above the ocean.

KEEPING *the* LIGHTS BURNING

Today British Columbia has one of the finest and most extensive systems of navigational lights in the world. Many of these are fully equipped light stations maintained by full-time resident keepers.

During the last few decades, one after another of the lighthouses elsewhere in Canada and throughout the United States have been automated. The lights at the top of the old towers still shine, but without the help of full-time keepers. Automatic timers, switches, and relays now do the work once done by human hands. Today the profession of lighthouse keeper is more or less extinct—except, that is, in British Columbia.

A Canadian keeper polishes the massive bull's-eye lens in the lantern room of a British Columbia lighthouse. Consisting of hundreds of separate glass prisms, Fresnel lenses concentrate light into a narrow band that can be seen for dozens of miles. Although highly effective, the lenses require meticulous care. (Photo by Chris Mills)

Many of the light stations on Canada's Pacific coast are so remote and yet so vital to shipping that it has long been felt necessary to keep a resident staff on hand for both routine maintenance and emergencies. This policy may be about to change, however. The Canadian government recently announced plans to automate British Columbia's remaining staffed lighthouses as an economy measure. Increasing pressure from maritime interests and tradition-minded British Columbians may cause the government to modify or abandon this plan. Otherwise, North America's last lighthouse keepers will lock the doors of their dwellings and leave for other jobs within the next few years.

"In my opinion, that will be a shame," says Chris Mills, the assistant keeper at Ivory Island Light Station on the famed Inside Passage.

A seven-year Canadian Coast Guard and lighthouse veteran, Mills served earlier at the Cross Island and Seal Island light stations in Nova Scotia. After those lights were automated, he transferred to British Columbia. "I've wanted to be a lighthouse keeper for as long as I can remember," he says.

While there is plenty of work to do around the station, the Ivory Island Light itself needs little keeping. Established in 1898, the lighthouse once had an enormous Fresnel lens, which required meticulous care and had to be hand polished nearly every day. But the old Fresnel has been gone for many years, its job taken over by a modern aero-marine beacon. Nonetheless, Mills and keeper Rene Kitson stay busy. There are logs to maintain, supplies to inventory, weather observations to take, and equipment to maintain, such as the diesel generator that powers the station's rotating beacon.

There are no roads in or out of Ivory Island. Diesel fuel and other supplies, as well as most of the station's groceries, are delivered once a month by Coast Guard tenders. Mail arrives every week or so via helicopter. About a year ago Mills married Seana Brackett, a former Nova Scotia nurse, and she now lives with him at the Ivory Island Station. Some would consider theirs an ideal existence; others might wonder how they deal with the isolation. The nearest community, Bella Bella, is about fifteen miles away by boat, far enough that Mills goes to town only two or three times a year.

"It can be lonely sometimes," says Mills. "But we don't feel isolated or cut off from civilization. In most ways, this is just like any other job."

Carol Slater, who shares keeping duties with her husband, Ian, at Race Rocks, one of British Columbia's oldest and most storied light stations, might not agree. The Slaters have been stationed at one lighthouse or another for twenty-seven years. They have lived at the Race Rocks Lighthouse, west of Victoria, for the past seven years. "We like to keep away from cities," says Carol Slater. "Here we can."

The Slaters became a lighthouse-keeping family in 1970. At that time Ian Slater's Coast Guard duties kept him apart from his wife and two children for months at a time. The Slaters wanted a more stable family life, so they turned to lighthouse keeping. "That way we were together nearly all the time," says Carol Slater.

Today the Slater's children are grown and have their own lives elsewhere, but Ian and Carol remain at Race Rocks. There they keep alive a profession and a tradition almost as old as civilization itself. Soon their way of life, the way of the lighthouse keeper, may be gone forever.

ATKINSON POINT LIGHT

West Vancouver, British Columbia – 1875 and 1910

Among the best-known structures in all of British Columbia is the Atkinson Point Lighthouse in West Vancouver. The hexagonal concrete tower is a favorite subject for photographers, who flock to nearby Lighthouse Viewpoint nearly every weekend. It is also much loved by seamen, who have followed its beacon for generations into Vancouver's bustling harbor.

Despite its fame, the lighthouse seen today is not the first to mark Atkinson Point. A wooden lighthouse was erected here in 1872 by Nanaimo contractor Arthur Finney, who billed the Canadian government $4,250 for the project. The light station did not go into service

immediately, however. The lighting apparatus, shipped thousands of miles from England, turned out to be the wrong size, and another had to be ordered. As a result the Atkinson Point Light did not shine until the evening of March 17, 1875, but it has rarely missed a night since.

After twenty-five years of service, the old lighthouse structures were demolished and a new concrete tower and two-story clapboard dwelling built in its place. Like several other lighthouse towers in storm- and earthquake-prone British Columbia, this one was reinforced with buttresses.

During World War II, Atkinson Point served as a billeting station for recruits and as the site for a shore battery. Huge searchlights were installed to scan the skies for enemy aircraft and the water for signs of submarine activity. But unlike the lighthouse at Estevan Point, the Atkinson Point Light never became a target for enemy fire. The battery on the point did manage to sink a ship, however. A warning shot fired to drive away local fishermen who had strayed into forbidden waters accidentally struck the *Fort Rae*, a friendly freighter recently launched from the nearby dry docks. The *Fort Rae* immediately took on water and had to be grounded by its astonished captain and crew.

Fisherman will find Atkinson Point a much friendlier and safer spot nowadays. Its lighthouse is made all the more attractive by its setting in the midst of a 185-acre park filled with virgin timber.

HOW TO GET THERE:

In West Vancouver follow Marine Drive toward Horseshoe Bay; take the turnoff into Lighthouse Park and follow the signs to the lighthouse. While in the area set aside plenty of time to explore Vancouver, the world-class city just across English Bay from the light. The zoo in Stanley Park is delightful, as are the Maritime Museum and Museum of Anthropology on Point Grey. Vancouver's Chinatown rivals the more famous oriental district of San Francisco. A map of the city is essential for visitors.

Atkinson Point Lighthouse keeps watch over English Bay and the entrance to Vancouver's bustling harbor. (Photo by Elaine Graham)

TRIAL ISLAND LIGHT

Victoria, British Columbia – 1906 and 1970

Just off Oak Bay at the far southeastern end of Vancouver Island, a barren rock more than half a mile long rises like a huge knife blade out of the Strait of Juan de Fuca. The rock is separated from the shore by Enterprise Channel, a narrow reach only about 300 feet wide. Currents running through the channel may top seven knots, and their strength and unpredictability make navigating these waters a trial. This may be the reason mariners long ago named the rock Trial Island. Others say the name devolved from the fact that wooden ships refitted at Victoria often made trial runs down the strait as far as the island to check their seaworthiness.

Whatever the source of its name, the rocky island has been a threat to shipping as long as mariners have sailed the strait. Dozens of vessels have met their end on or near the island. In 1891 the tug *Emma* tore out her bottom and sank while trying to pass through Enterprise Channel. Four years later the tug *Velos* and freighter *Pilot*, hauling stone blocks for construction of government buildings in Victoria, foundered while trying to traverse the channel in a storm. At least eight lives were lost in the disaster. Even the survey ship *Egeria*, sent to Trial Island in 1898 to size it up as a likely site for a lighthouse, ran aground there before its task was complete.

The Canadian government completed construction of a lighthouse on Trial Island in 1906. A rectangular, three-story combination dwelling and tower, it was located near the far south end of the island, where the bare rock reaches its maximum elevation of approximately fifty feet. The building was approximately thirty feet square and the tower thirty-four feet high. The station was equipped with a Fresnel lens displaying a flashing beacon and a diaphonic fog signal. The flashing light could be seen from fifteen miles at sea. Only days before the light and signal were placed in regular service, the steamer *Twickenham* got lost in a heavy fog and struck the rock. Both

the *Twickenham* and its sweet cargo of 5,000 tons of sugar were successfully salvaged.

Originally, the lantern room peeked through the roof of the dwelling, but in 1970 a separate tower was built in front of the original lighthouse. The new lantern room received an aero-marine–type lighting apparatus, and the old lantern and Fresnel lens were removed and placed in Victoria's Bastion Square. There, to the special delight of children and tourists, the old light still flashes each night.

HOW TO GET THERE:

Trial Island can only be reached by boat, and its lighthouse is not usually open to the public. As of 1997 this lighthouse still had resident keepers, but the facility may be automated in the near future. Bastion Square is located near the center of Victoria, between Government and Wharf Streets. The lantern and Fresnel lens that served at Trial Island for more than sixty years are located in the square, near the Maritime Museum of British Columbia.

FISGARD LIGHT

Victoria, British Columbia – 1860

On a small, rocky island at the entrance to Esquimalt Harbor near Victoria stands Fisgard, one of the most historic and impressive lighthouses in North America. Fisgard is one of Canada's famed "Imperial Lights," originally funded by the British Empire's Board of Trade.

Built of iron, granite, brick, heavy western timbers, and other solid stuff, it was completed and lit in the fall of 1860, making it British Columbia's first official lighthouse.

The fifty-six-foot tower and two-story keeper's dwelling, both of early Victorian design, were the work of

Prim and stately, the Victorian Fisgard Lighthouse marks Esquimalt Harbor near Victoria, the tradition-conscious capital of British Columbia.

John Wright, the same contractor who built some of the colony's government buildings. Wright built Fisgard to last, giving it a two-foot-thick granite foundation and fortresslike four-foot-thick brick walls. The brick used in construction was imported from England, as were the iron fittings and lighting apparatus that were installed atop the fifty-six-foot cylindrical tower. The lantern and machinery needed to drive the rotating light cost an estimated 2,800 pounds sterling (the equivalent at the time of about $14,000 in U.S. currency).

Fisgard's first keeper was also an import. Hired at a rate of 150 pounds per year to maintain and operate the light, George Davies set sail from England early in 1860 on a six-month voyage that would take him and his young family halfway around the world. Accompanying Davies were the reflectors, fittings, and other equipment needed to convert the empty shell of the Fisgard tower into a true, working lighthouse. By the late fall Davies had everything necessary installed, and on the evening of November 16, 1860, the flashing Fisgard beacon was seen for the first time.

To produce the signal, a series of catoptric reflectors were arrayed on a turntable around the lamp. As the table rotated, each reflector in turn produced a bright flash of light. Originally the lamp burned vegetable or dogfish oil. Later the lamps burned kerosene, a much more reliable and efficient fuel. More efficient, too, was the Fresnel lens that replaced the reflectors during the 1880s. The Fisgard station used tinted panes to produce its characteristic red, white, and green flashes. The colors and flashes helped distinguish the light from the fixed white beacons of its American neighbors across the Strait of Juan de Fuca.

The lighthouse takes its name from the British frigate *HMS Fisgard*, which served the Royal Navy in the Northwest during the 1840s. The name is derived from an old Viking name, *Fiskegaart*.

Fisgard was among the first British Columbian lights to be automated. The last full-time keeper left the station in 1929. The old Fresnel lens is gone, replaced by an aeromarine beacon, but the light remains operational. Today the lighthouse serves as a key attraction of the Fort Rodd Hill and Fisgard Lighthouse National Historic Site. The fort consists of a series of shore batteries built during the late 1800s.

HOW TO GET THERE:

The fort and lighthouse are located on the west side of Esquimalt Harbor, about 6 miles west of downtown Victoria. Follow Highway 1A West and then turn left onto Fort Rodd Hill Road. The Fort Rodd Hill and Fisgard Lighthouse National Historic Site is open from 10:00 A.M. to 5:30 P.M. daily, although services are limited from November through February. Self-guided tours, interpretive displays, and audiovisual programs recount the rich history of the lighthouse and the fort. For more information call (604) 478–5849 or fax (604) 478–2816.

Visitors should set aside plenty of time to explore the old colonial city of Victoria, the capital of British Columbia. A charming business district reminiscent of old London and world-class museums and parks make Victoria a one-of-a-kind experience. Ferries connect Victoria to Vancouver, Seattle, and Port Angeles on the Olympic Peninsula.

RACE ROCKS LIGHT

Sooke, British Columbia – 1860

The Imperial Light on Race Rocks, just off the far southern toe of Vancouver Island, first shined on the evening of December 26, 1860. Had it been in service only three days earlier, it might have saved the hapless *Nanette*, a three-masted freighter bearing a highly valuable cargo from Europe.

The Race Rocks Light, intended to mark one of the most dangerous navigational obstacles in western North America, had been scheduled to begin service early in the fall of 1860. Its sister light, Fisgard, just outside of nearby Esquimalt Harbour, had shined brightly since mid-November, but construction delays and equipment

As rugged as its setting, the granite Race Rocks Light tower has stood through countless howling Northwestern gales.

problems put off the lighting of the lamps at the Race Rocks station until far into December.

With his captain ill with dysentery, First Mate William McCulloch was in command as the *Nanette* entered the Strait of Juan de Fuca on the evening of December 22. McCulloch had been told the threatening rocks would be marked by a major navigational light. Seeing only the Fisgard Light, McCulloch mistakenly believed he was far out in the strait and allowed the *Nanette* to drift toward what he imagined would be safe harbor at Victoria. Instead, at first light, he found the *Nanette* had drifted in amongst the ship-killing Race Rocks. There was no wind to help McCulloch sail his ship out of danger, and the *Nanette* soon struck hard on a rock and began to sink. Although fatally damaged and awash in the waves, she became hung up on the shoals and did not disappear from sight until nearly three months later.

With the help of lighthouse personnel, all hands aboard the *Nanette* reached shore safely. But salvaging the *Nanette's* cargo of oil, blankets, shoes, saddles, oakum, twine, and other merchandise, worth up to $170,000, would prove daunting. News of all those goods available for salvage raised an uproar in communities up and down the coast of British Columbia and on the American side of the strait as well. Frenzied treasure seekers hurried to the wreck in small boats, while others combed nearby shores for drifting boxloads of cargo. Since there was a sizable quantity of whiskey, gin, and ale in the *Nanette's* holds, some salvagers spent as much time imbibing as they did working. The *Victoria Colonist* described the turmoil as follows:

The scene among the wreckers is said to baffle description. Disputes as to the possession of packages fished up are constantly taking place, and not a few rough and tumble fights. . . . Every one seems to be working on his own hook, and in every case demands salvage for what he brings up. . . . A great deal of drinking and rowdyism is going on at the wreck, and black eyes and broken noses are quite fashionable there.

Ironically, by the time the *Nanette* finally slipped off the rocks and beneath the waves on February 26, 1861, the Race Rocks Light had been in smooth and continuous operation for two full months. During its early months of service, keeper George Davies did double duty, watching over the light by night and painting the tower by day. The gray granite tower so closely resembled the rocks of the mainland behind it that mariners tended to lose sight of it during the day. To make the tower stand out, Davies hauled himself up in a bosun's chair and painted the tower in alternating black and white stripes.

A marvel of engineering, the tower was designed in England, its stones cut to size by Scottish quarrymen and then shipped to British Columbia for reassembly at Race Rocks. Since the stones had been carefully numbered, on-site construction was supposed to have been a simple matter of stacking and cementing stones. The process proved confusing, however, and the difficulty of hoisting the heavy stones into place delayed construction and, perhaps, doomed the *Nanette*.

The light and fog signal at Race Rocks did not put an end to shipping disasters in the area. More than a few fog-bound vessels succumbed to a mysterious "silent zone" that somehow prevented their pilots from hearing the blast of the Race Rocks fog horn. While the signal could be deafening on either side of the zone, within it mariners might hear little but the engines of their own ship. Many such vessels were lost practically within shouting distance of the lighthouse and its foghorns. Maritime investigators eventually concluded that a bizarre deflection of the sound waves by the surrounding rocks and the tower itself had created the silent zone. To correct the problem, the foghorns were mounted on a separate tower some distance from the lighthouse.

HOW TO GET THERE:

From Victoria follow Highway 1A West, Highway 14, and Happy Valley Road. Turn right onto Rocky Point Road and follow it to the Pedder Bay Marina. Here it is possible to rent a boat for the fifteen- to twenty-minute voyage to the Race Rocks Lighthouse. For information on prices and seasonal availability of rentals, write the Pedder Bay Marina, 925 Pedder Bay Drive, RR #2 Victoria, B.C. V9B 5B4 or call (604) 478–1771.

ESTEVAN POINT LIGHT

Estevan Point, British Columbia – 1910

At Estevan Point, far up the rugged Pacific-facing coast of Vancouver Island, stands one of the most remarkable structures in western North America. With its flying concrete buttresses, the 150-foot tower of the Estevan Point Lighthouse has an ultramodern look.

Despite its space rocket–like appearance, the freestanding concrete structure was completed nine decades ago, only a few years into the twentieth century.

The crews who built this extraordinary tower had no access to roads and only limited tools. Supply problems,

(Photo by Dave and Louise Edgington)

rotten food, bad weather, and trouble with local Indians delayed construction so that the project, begun early in 1907, was not finished until 1910. All materials and what little machinery was available were brought in by ship. Since there was no safe anchorage near the construction site, supplies and equipment were brought ashore at the Hesquiat Indian village about five miles away. Before any work on the station itself could be done, a trail had to be cleared and a track laid over miles of rocky terrain so that supplies could be brought to the site by mule-drawn rail car.

At first the Hesquiat people were friendly to the construction effort, but the disruption of their traditional lifestyle and the disfigurement of their ancestral lands soon generated deep resentments. In May 1908 their anger boiled over as a Hesquiat chief led a small band on a raid, destroying several buildings filled with supplies. Peace was soon restored, but afterwards, relations with the Hesquiats were never congenial and were frequently strained.

In November 1908 a Pacific gale tore up 200 yards of irreplaceable track, forcing members of the construction crew to carry supplies in on their backs or in small man-powered carts. For months at a time, heavy rains made progress on the tower next to impossible. But despite all these difficulties, the station was finally completed and ready for operation by February 1910.

The lantern atop the Estevan Point tower received the finest and most powerful lighting apparatus available: a first-order Fresnel lens. It was so large that a man could

spread his arms inside it without touching any of its glass prisms. A rotating bull's-eye lens, the big Fresnel concentrated light into powerful flashes, which could be seen by mariners more than twenty miles out into the Pacific. Together with frames, housing, turntable, and dome, the station's iron lantern weighed twenty-five tons. The lens alone cost $35,000.

The concrete tower was designed to withstand gales and even earthquakes. A series of spreading buttresses help support the central cylinder, which encloses a spiral iron staircase with 150 steps. In high wind or when shaken by tremors, the tower can sway from side to side with minimal damage. As a consequence, it has survived two earthquakes and innumerable storms and remains, today, as solid as ever.

The Estevan Point Station was the only lighthouse in North America to fall under enemy attack during World War II. In June of 1942, with war raging through much of the Pacific, a Japanese submarine surfaced off the point and fired at least twenty-five shells at the tower. The barrage did surprisingly little damage, but some of the shells passed over the tower and exploded in the village beyond. Enraged Hesquiats piled into their boats, and if the Japanese had not slipped away under cover of a smoke screen, theirs might have become the only submarine in history to be attacked by Indians.

Estevan Point and its lighthouse are named for the tender *Estevan*, which brought welcome supplies to light stations throughout British Columbia early in the twentieth century. It remains in operation and is considered one of British Columbia's and North America's most important lights.

Few roads penetrate the wild northwestern coast of Vancouver Island, and access to the lighthouse is limited.

Estevan Point Light Station was the target of a World War II submarine attack. The concrete tower survived the shelling just as it has numerous assaults by Pacific storms. (Photo by Dave and Louise Edgington)

A Canadian Coast Guard helicopter brings mail, food, and supplies to isolated Ivory Island Lighthouse. British Columbia has few main roads, and remote coastal stations like this one may be a hundred miles or more from the nearest truck or shopping mall parking lot. As are many of Western Canada's light stations, the Ivory Island Light is maintained by resident keepers—among the last in North America. (Photo by Chris Mills)

CHAPTER FOUR

Lights on
THE ROOF OF THE WORLD
ALASKA

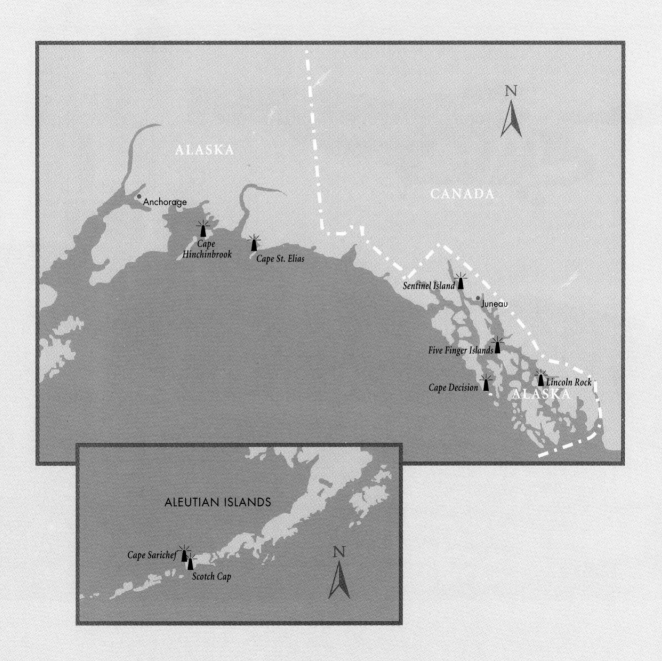

A U.S. Coast Guard chopper lands at Cape Decision Lighthouse overlooking Chatham Strait. Like Alaska's other lighthouses, this one has long been automated, but periodic maintenance visits remain necessary. (Courtesy U.S. Coast Guard)

laska's coastline is longer than that of all the rest of the states put together. Of America's 12,383 miles of coast, some 6,740 miles, or approximately 55 percent, is Alaskan. When all its thousands of bays, inlets, estuaries, passages, reaches, straits, and islands are taken into consideration, Alaska boasts an incredible 33,904 miles of shoreline. Obviously, people in search of waterfront property should try Alaska—that is, if they are tough enough.

These are not gentle shores. While the fishing is the best anywhere and the scenery unimaginably beautiful, Alaska is no place for the faint of heart. Neither are its waters. Strewn with rocks, some of them still uncharted, mined with icebergs, and frequently blanketed by fog or torn by ferocious storms, the seas off Alaska are some of the most treacherous on the planet. Every year dozens of vessels run into trouble here. Some simply disappear and are never heard from again. Yet Alaska's thousands of miles of dangerous coast are guarded by a relative handful of major lighthouses—about sixteen—fewer, in fact, than those that light the 200-mile coast of Massachusetts.

THE FIRST NORTHERN LIGHTS

The maritime history of the Far Northwest got off to an ominous beginning in 1741, when Danish adventurer Vitus Bering explored Alaska, claiming it for his employer, the Russian czar. On his way back to Siberia, Bering fell victim to shipwreck. Countless thousands of the brave mariners who eventually followed Bering to these waters would suffer a similar fate. Russian fur-trading vessels ran aground and wrecked along Alaska's deadly coast with clocklike regularity. There were almost never any survivors, and in any case, no relief ships were sent out to rescue them. Russian captains had access to only the most rudimentary charts and could rely on only one recognized navigational light along the entire coast. It shined from the cupola of a castlelike structure overlooking the harbor of Sitka, the Russian capital of Alaska.

Even after the Americans took control of Alaska in 1867, the U.S. government expended little or no effort to make it a safer place for sailors. As with much of the American Northwest and British Columbia, the need for lights along the Alaskan coast was largely ignored until the early twentieth century. The high cost of building and maintaining even a rudimentary system of lights and lifesaving stations was considered prohibitive. But it was not just negligence and budgetary stinginess that caused Congress to look away from Alaska when it came time to vote funds for new lighthouses. It was long believed—and to an extent it is still thought—to be impossible to properly light this remote and rugged coast, longer than that of most nations.

The 1896 Klondike Gold Strike touched off a wild northward rush of treasure hunters and brought a sharp increase in traffic along the dangerous Alaskan coast. Entire boatloads of gold seekers were lost in storms and shipwrecks before they ever reached the Klondike. Many of those who did strike it rich lost their lives on the way back home and never got to enjoy their new wealth. In 1898 the steamer *Clara Nevada* tore open her hull on jagged Eldred Rock and went to the bottom, carrying with her more than a hundred miners and dozens of sacks of Klondike gold. While steaming past Douglass Island in 1901, the gold-laden *Islander* struck an iceberg and sank, along with forty-two passengers and crew.

Faced with carnage on this scale, Congress at long last took action and funded the first of Alaska's major lighthouses—Five Fingers Island and Sentinel Island, both completed and in service by the end of 1902. In rapid succession there followed the Scotch Cap, Mary Island, and Lincoln Rock stations in 1903, Tree Point, Fairway Island, Guard Islands, Point Retreat, Cape Sarichef, and Point Sherman in 1904, and Eldred Rock in 1906. Later came Cape Hinchinbrook (1910), Cape St. Elias (1916), Cape Spencer (1925), and Cape Decision (1932). The protection provided by these fully staffed, primary light and fog stations was bolstered by hundreds of minor facilities, most of them small gaslights that could burn unattended for many weeks between visits by Lighthouse Service tenders. Mariners could now expect to be guided by lights, at least along some of the more dangerous stretches of Alaskan coast.

A blanket of snow covers Cape St. Elias Light Station near the entrance to Alaska's famed Prince William Sound. Completed in 1916, the light marked what many seaman considered the most dangerous point along the entire Alaskan coast. (Courtesy U.S. Coast Guard)

ON *the* ROOF *of* HELL

Alaska's lighthouses rank among the most remote outposts, not just in the United States or North America, but in all the world. Nowadays Alaska's lights are automated, and they do their important work of guiding ships and saving lives without the help of human hands. Until recently, however, many of these lights required constant attention and maintenance, so keepers had to live at the stations year-round. These keepers could not have found lonelier jobs. For some, the nearest town might be dozens, or even hundreds, of miles away. Many of Alaska's light stations were men-only facilities, meaning that keepers might be separated from family and friends for a year or more at a time. Their work was dangerous, too. More than a few of Alaska's lighthouse keepers lost their lives in the line of duty.

No Alaskan light stations were more isolated than those at Scotch Cap and Cape Sarichef, both on Unimak Island in the Aleutians. Completed and placed in service in 1903 and 1904 respectively, the two lighthouses guided vessels through the narrow passage linking the open Pacific Ocean with the Bering Sea. Believing it to be haunted, Aleutian natives referred to Unimak Island as "the roof of hell," but the lighthouse keepers stationed here were more inclined to think of it as "the end of the earth."

The island was so remote that during the early part of the century, lighthouse tenders visited it only once a year at most. Keepers served here for up to three years and then were given a year of leave to help them reestablish their ties with the civilized world. Once the Coast Guard took custody of America's lighthouses, tours of duty at Scotch Cap, Cape Sarichef, and other such isolated stations were limited to one year. Even so, a year can be a very long time in a place where the nearest neighbors for dozens of miles are polar bears.

For five young Coast Guardsmen posted here just after World War II, their year on Unimak became an eternity. Their names were Jack Colvin, Paul Ness, Leonard Pickering, Anthony Pettit, and Dewey Dykstra. Only one of the five—it has never been clear which—was awake, keeping watch over the vital Scotch Cap Light, when an earthquake struck shortly after 1:30 A.M. on April 1, 1946. The shock tumbled the four sleepers out of their beds, and they quickly joined their on-duty comrade to check the station for damage. Likely as not, they only found a little—some broken dishes, equipment displaced, lockers thrown open, and that sort of thing. But no one was about to go back to bed. Something strange was happening. Water was draining out of Unimak Pass and away from the island and rushing out toward the Pacific. Shortly after 2:15 that morning the five keepers must have thought nature was playing some monstrous April Fool's joke on them— that is, if they had time to think at all—once they saw what had happened to all that water. It had been sucked up into a tidal wave, at least one hundred feet high, and it was barreling toward them at 500 miles per hour. There was no escape.

According to the crew of a direction-finding station located far up on the Unimak Island cliffs, the tsunami struck the lighthouse at 2:18 A.M. By the time the sea had calmed, only the foundation of the reinforced concrete building was left. The crew of the direction-finding station survived the disaster and eventually located the bodies of the five keepers after they washed up on the shore of Unimak Island.

A small memorial at Scotch Cap honors the victims of the 1946 earthquake and tidal wave. But the true memorial to the keepers who perished here is the Scotch Cap light itself. Automated in 1971, it still guides mariners trying to pass safely along Alaska's deadly coast.

LINCOLN ROCK LIGHT

Clarence Strait, Alaska – 1903

Few lighthouse stations have proved as difficult to establish and maintain as the one on Lincoln Rock, a tiny, barren island near the western end of the Clarence Strait, some fifty-four miles northwest of Ketchikan, Alaska. Funded in 1902, the project got off to a shaky start when the construction contractor lost a small steamer, a barge, and a large load of lumber in a gale. No doubt financially strapped, the contractor tried to recoup his losses by using substandard materials and was eventually fired by the Lighthouse Service.

Purchasing its own materials, the service hired laborers and completed the station in time for an official lighting on December 1, 1903. A short square tower pushed through the roof of the two-story wooden keeper's dwelling. The lantern room contained a fourth-order Fresnel lens, which displayed a fixed white light.

Much of the tiny island is submerged at high tide, so the lighthouse was built atop a concrete pier to protect it from the waves. As it turned out, however, the building was much more exposed than was at first thought. Large storm-driven waves often broke over the pier, smashing into the side of the dwelling. By 1909 the lighthouse had been so badly damaged by wave action that it had to be abandoned. It was never completely rebuilt.

In 1911 a manned fog-signal station went into service about a quarter of a mile from the old pier. An automated acetylene light took the place of the original beacon. The Lincoln Rock Station was permanently discontinued in 1968.

The site of the Lincoln Rock Lighthouse is not accessible to the public.

This old photograph, probably taken during the 1950s, shows Lincoln Rock Lighthouse during its active years. The station was discontinued in 1968. (Courtesy U.S. Coast Guard)

CAPE DECISION LIGHT

Cape Decision, Alaska – 1932

During the early decades of the twentieth century, the fishing industry in Alaska burgeoned, especially in the panhandle region. Salmon canneries, herring-salting facilities, and reduction plants multiplied on the shores of the Chatham and Sumner Straits and among the islands forming the seaward wall of the Inside Passage. Countless fishing boats traveled back and forth through the foggy narrows separating the islands. Often they passed by Cape Decision on the far southeastern end of Kuiu Island, about sixty miles from the old Russian settle-

(Courtesy U.S. Coast Guard)

ment of Sitka. Here the masters of vessels moving northward through the panhandle must choose between several likely routes. Here, too, they face an assortment of dangers, including strong tides, hidden rocks, and unpredictable weather as well as the ubiquitous coastal fog.

For years seaman near the cape had to rely for guidance on an unwatched acetylene light that shined from one of the Spanish Islands near the cape, but most considered it woefully inadequate. Their pleas for a better, more powerful light fell on deaf ears in the tightfisted Congress of the 1920s. Finally, only a few months before the Stock Market Crash of 1929 and the beginning of the Great Depression, Congress relented and approved partial funding for a lighthouse on Cape Decision.

The isolation of the site, funding shortages during the early years of the Depression, and the cape's notoriously foul weather all hindered progress. After three years of start-and-stop construction, the lighthouse was finally completed in 1932 at a total cost of $158,000 and placed in service on March 15 of that year.

The station's square, forty-foot tower rose from the flat roof of the main, reinforced concrete building. Its flashing, 350,000-candlepower light reached out to mariners from an elevation of ninety-six feet. During the fog and heavy weather that frequently blankets the cape, an especially powerful fog signal warned vessels away from nearby rocks. A radio beacon helped guide ships in from the open Pacific.

The station had quarters for at least three resident keepers. As with most of Alaska's lighthouse keepers, theirs was a lonely existence. The monotony was broken by trips to nearby Port Alexander, the sporadic visits of supply tenders, and by fishing and hunting expeditions, which had the added benefit of placing fresh meat on the station table. After a year of service, keepers received a ninety-day leave.

Supplies were landed in a narrow protected ravine, lifted onto the rocks by a hoist, and then transferred to the lighthouse by means of an elevated tramway. The station's boathouse and a portion of the tram were destroyed in a 1989 fire. Automated in 1974, the Cape Decision Light remains in service.

The Cape Decision Lighthouse is inaccessible to the public.

The rain-and-rust-streaked walls of the Cape Decision Lighthouse show how the station is constantly at war with the ocean. Although it has quarters for three resident keepers, the automated lighthouse stands its vigil alone. (Courtesy U.S. Coast Guard)

FIVE FINGER ISLANDS LIGHT

Five Finger Islands, Alaska – 1902 and 1935

One of Alaska's first two official lighthouses, the Five Finger Islands Light Station was established just after the turn of the twentieth century to guide ships through the Inside Passage to Juneau. Located on a craggy island in the northern section of Frederick Sound north of Petersburg, its beacon first shined on March 1, 1902, the same night the Sentinel Island Light was placed in service.

A two-story combination dwelling and tower, the original Five Finger Islands Lighthouse displayed a fixed white light focused by a fourth-order Fresnel lens. The lantern room peeked through the roof of the structure, its light shining from a point sixty-eight feet above high water. A wooden structure, the lighthouse served for more than thirty years before it burned to the ground in December 1933.

The government moved quickly to restore this vital Inside Passage light station, and a new lighthouse was completed and in operation by late in 1935. This one was built to last and to this day continues to guide ships, ferries, and fishing boats plying the waters of the passage. Standing on a hefty concrete pier, the forty-foot-square main building is itself built of reinforced concrete. It serves as a platform for the sixty-eight-foot tower, which places the station's light more than eighty feet above the water.

The keepers who served at this station shared the building with boilers, batteries, and a jumble of other equipment. The Five Finger Islands Station remained fully staffed longer than any Alaskan lighthouse. The last full-time keepers left the station in 1984, bringing to a close a unique era in lighthouse history.

HOW TO GET THERE:

The light can be seen from the decks of the ferries that travel the extraordinarily scenic Inside Passage. Otherwise, like most other Alaskan lighthouses, it is inaccessible to the public.

Five Finger Islands Light Station as it appeared in 1929. The light was automated in 1984. (Courtesy U.S. Coast Guard)

Standing against a backdrop of towering peaks and tall forests, the Sentinel Island Lighthouse is graced by a spectacular setting rivaling any in North America. Among Alaska's earliest light stations, it was established in 1902 to guide vessels into the Lynn Canal northwest of Juneau. The residence, where keepers lived a rustic and solitary existence for a year or more at a time, was torn down after the light was automated in 1966. Today the station remains in operation but needs little human assistance. Solar panels help charge the batteries that supply electric power for the light and fog signal. (Courtesy U.S. Coast Guard)

CAPE SPENCER LIGHT

Cape Spencer, Alaska – 1925

The keepers of Cape Spencer Lighthouse must have thought they were living at the end of the earth. Located on a barren, rocky island at the entrance to Cross Sound on the northern end of the Alaska panhandle, this duty station placed keepers a half-day round-trip journey from mail or services of any kind. The nearest town, Juneau, was more than seventy miles away.

As early as 1906 commercial maritime interests had pressed the Lighthouse Service for a light to mark the cape and the route through Icy Strait often followed by vessels trying to avoid the stormy Outside Passage. At that time, however, service resources were stretched to the limit, and it was not until 1913 that a small, automated acetylene beacon was placed on the cape.

Construction of a fully operational light station began in 1923 atop a precipitous, exposed rock just off the tip of the cape. The isolation and ruggedness of the site drove the cost of the facility to more than $175,000. Completed in 1925, it consisted of a fourteen-foot-wide square tower rising twenty-five feet above the flat roof of a reinforced concrete fog-signal building, which also served as a residence for the keepers. A steel derrick and gasoline-powered hoist lifted supplies from a small landing to the lighthouse, which stood at the top of the rock, about eighty feet above the sea.

The lantern displays a flashing white light with a focal plane 105 feet above the water. The station also guides vessels with an exceptionally powerful radio beacon, often received by ships as many as 200 miles from shore.

Wayne Wheeler, president of the U.S. Lighthouse Society, once served on the Coast Guard cutter *Sweetbrier*, which provided logistical support to Cape Spencer and other panhandle lighthouses. The Cape Spencer Light has been automated since 1974.

HOW TO GET THERE:

The Cape Spencer Lighthouse is, of course, inaccessible from land and is off limits to the public. Often it can be seen from a distance by passengers on cruise ships visiting Glacier Bay National Park. Planes offering scenic tours of Glacier Bay operate out of Juneau during warmer weather months and occasionally fly near the lighthouse.

(Courtesy U.S. Coast Guard)

This unusual octagonal lighthouse stands on Eldred Rock, south of Haines and Skagway at the northwestern end of the Alaska panhandle. The tower rises through the roof of the dwelling, placing the focal plane of the light more than ninety feet above the water. The light guides ships along the strategic Lynn Canal. (Courtesy U.S. Coast Guard)

CAPE ST. ELIAS LIGHT

Cape St. Elias, Alaska – 1916

The masters of ships emerging from the open Pacific off the southern coast of Alaska often search the horizon for a rocky fist thrusting skyward. The fist, a 1,700-foot peak known as Mount St. Elias, can be seen rising above the clouds even when fog blankets the coastline. Mariners bound for Prince William Sound or the Cook Inlet use St. Elias as a daymark pointing the way to safer, calmer waters beyond.

Ironically, the mountain and the waters around it are by no means safe. In fact, Cape St. Elias is considered by many seamen to be the most dangerous spot along the entire Pacific coast of North America. As if to warn against the threat, mysterious colored lights are said to play along the shores here. Some say a sea monster lurks in the bays and inlets near the mountain. More certain, however, are the monstrous qualities of nearby shoals and rocks, which have torn open the hulls of more vessels than anyone can count.

Reflecting an early general neglect of Alaska by the federal government, few lighthouses were built along its 6,740 miles of coastline (more than half the U.S. total) until the twentieth century. Funds for a lighthouse to guide ships through the perilous waters off Cape St. Elias were not approved until 1913. One year earlier the lighthouse tender *Armeria* had wrecked while on route to place a buoy here. Embarrassed by the incident, maritime officials quickly resolved to establish a permanent light station somewhere near the cape, and by the fall of 1916,

Like other Alaskan light stations, the Cape St. Elias Lighthouse continues its task of guiding mariners without the help of a resident keeper. A bank of solar panels below the lantern gives its batteries a boost. (Courtesy U.S. Coast Guard)

the lighthouse was complete. Its 300,000-candlepower light was first displayed on the evening of September 16.

The Cape St. Elias station consisted of a fifty-five-foot-tall reinforced concrete tower rising from the corner of a fog-signal building, a two-story keeper's dwelling, a boathouse, and storage buildings. It was so isolated and so difficult to reach that supply ships arrived only once a year. Usually, only men served here, and forced to remain at the station for a year or more at a time, keepers often found their existence at Cape St. Elias an oppressively con-fining one. Some keepers considered this the "worst light-house duty station in America," and it is easy to see why. Fresh meat and vegetables were rarely seen on the dinner table at this lighthouse. Keepers sometimes found themselves vying with the gulls for fish that had been marooned by the tides on the rocks below the lighthouse. Mail, delivered by passing boats, arrived sporadically. The storms that blew up off the cape were often so powerful that rocks, kelp, and small fish were thrown up into the lantern room. The mountain behind the station posed other dangers as, occasionally, huge boulders came tumbling down its precipitous slopes and crashing through the trees. No doubt, few of the keepers who had served at Cape St. Elias were sorry to hear that the station was decommissioned in 1974 and replaced by a small automated light.

Despite its considerable power, the light at Cape St. Elias was never particularly effective. The beacon was often obscured by fog, and the relatively low eighty-five-foot elevation of its focal plane limited its range to only about fifteen miles. To help guide mariners, a radio beacon was installed here in 1927.

The lighthouse is inaccessible to the public.

Wearing the Lighthouse Service uniform, assistant Cape St. Elias keeper Ted Pedersen stands in front of his lighthouse in 1927. Alaskan light-houses were so remote that keepers had to remain on station for a year or more at a time. Some could not bear the isolation, while others, like Pedersen, relished it. (Courtesy U.S. Coast Guard)

CAPE HINCHINBROOK LIGHT

Hinchinbrook Island, Alaska – 1910 and 1934

In all the world there are few more beautiful or more economically vital ocean inlets than Prince William Sound. Walled in by rock, forest, and mountain, its crystal waters teem with salmon, seals, sea otters, and seabirds of every description. The sound is a northern paradise. It is also a highway for supertankers as long as three football fields and for cruise ships that come here so their passengers can relish the sound's beauty.

At the head of Prince William Sound is the strategic port of Valdez, the terminus of the Alaska Oil Pipeline. Valdez plays host to more tankers than any port this side of the Persian Gulf, and it is for this reason, among others,

The modernistic, reinforced-concrete design of the Cape Hinchinbrook Lighthouse was intended less for looks than to enable the structure to withstand earthquakes. A major tremor destroyed the previous tower six years before this one was completed in 1934. (Courtesy U.S. Coast Guard)

that the Cape Hinchinbrook Lighthouse, which marks the entrance of the sound, is one of the most important navigational markers in operation today.

Hinchinbrook Island and its southwestward-thrusting cape have been recognized as key seamarks for as long as oceangoing vessels have visited Alaska. (Russian ships started coming here in the 1740s.) The Lighthouse Service considered placing a light on the cape as early as 1900 but could not coax funds from a reluctant Congress, struggling even then to balance the annual federal budget. Only after the wreck of the steamer *Oregon* on the island's merciless rocks in 1906 was money voted for the project. In order not to rock their own budget boat, Congress provided the money in stages, setting aside a portion of the necessary funds each year until the required $125,000 had been raised and finally became available in 1909.

In April 1909 contractor A. B. Lewis of Seattle brought a crew of forty men to Hinchinbrook Island, hoping to complete the station that same year. But as was often the case with construction projects in Alaska, the weather played havoc with the schedule. Rain and wind halted work at Cape Hinchinbrook for weeks at a time. An especially powerful storm washed away a scow loaded with supplies valued at $12,000. By September, when construction had to be suspended because of dwindling light and increasing cold, only the station's wharf and tramway had been completed. Nine months later work on the station resumed, and this time, it went quickly. By the fall the tower and other structures were in place, and on the evening of November 15, 1910, the station's light began its nightly task of guiding ships.

The light and fog signal were housed in an octagonal concrete building more than fifty feet in diameter. Equipped with a third-order Fresnel lens of an advanced design said to provide the same power as a first-order lens,

the lantern stood atop the two-story roof. Shining from an elevation of almost 200 feet, its light could be seen from as many as twenty-five miles at sea.

The lighthouse was of such advanced design and so solidly built that some thought it to be "indestructible." Such notions were popular during the early twentieth century. For instance, the liner *Titanic* was thought to be "unsinkable" before its fatal encounter with a North Atlantic iceberg less than two years after the Cape Hinchinberg Lighthouse went into service. The lighthouse outlasted the *Titanic* by more than a decade, but in time proved just as vulnerable to the destructive power of nature. In 1927 and again in 1928, earthquakes rocked the station, cracking concrete walls, breaking up the foundation, and threatening to dump the entire structure, along with the cliff on which it stood, into the Pacific.

Alarmed by the damage, the Light Service decided to build another light tower on Cape Hinchinbrook, this time on a more stable foundation of solid rock. Completed in 1934, the reinforced-concrete structure rises sixty-seven feet above the cliff and displays a powerful light supplied by the station's original third-order lens. Although no one has claimed it indestructible, this lighthouse is still guiding ships today, more than six decades after it was placed in service. Along with several other Alaskan lights, this one was automated in 1974.

HOW TO GET THERE:

The lighthouse is inaccessible to the public. However, it can sometimes be seen from the deck of cruise ships, ferries, and other vessels entering or exiting Prince William Sound.

SCOTCH CAP LIGHT

Unimak Island, Alaska – 1903 and 1950

The original Scotch Cap Lighthouse was an octagonal wooden structure located on the side of a cliff about ninety feet above the sea. Built for a total of $76,571 by a team of thirty workers brought from Seattle, the tower and other station facilities took more than a year to complete. Placed in operation on July 15, 1903, it displayed a flashing white light produced by a third-order Fresnel lens.

In 1940 the old wooden lighthouse was replaced by a reinforced concrete structure. Ironically, it was this new, much sturdier building that was smashed and swept away by the tsunami of 1946 (see the introduction to this chapter).

A replacement facility was ready for duty by 1950. Built far up on the cliff to keep it safe from future tidal waves, the new lighthouse bore little resemblance to its predecessors. A rugged, rectangular concrete structure, it looks more like a storage building than a lighthouse. A rotating aero-marine beacon shines from atop its flat roof 116 feet above the sea. Since the facility is fully automated, no personnel are stationed at Scotch Cap today.

(We're joking, right?) The Scotch Cap Lighthouse is inaccessible to the public.

The Scotch Cap Lighthouse as it looked before a tidal wave smashed it in 1946. (Courtesy U.S. Coast Guard)

Clinging to the "roof of hell," on bleak Unimak Island in the Aleutians, Cape Sarichef Lighthouse is the most westerly lighthouse in North America. Automated since 1950, the station dates to 1904, when it was placed here to guide ships through Unimak Pass, which links the Pacific Ocean with the Bering Sea. (Courtesy U.S. Coast Guard)

LIGHTHOUSES INDEX

Numerals in italics indicate photograph/legend only.

BIBLIOGRAPHY

Adams, William Henry Davenport. *Lighthouses and Lightships: A Descriptive and Historical Account of Their Mode of Construction and Organization.* New York: Scribner's, 1870.

Adamson, Hans Christian. *Keepers of the Light.* New York: Greenberg, 1955.

Beaver, Patrick. *A History of Lighthouses.* Secaucus, N.J.: Citadel, 1972.

Chase, Mary Ellen. *The Story of Lighthouses.* New York: Norton, 1965.

Gibbs, Jim. *Lighthouses of the Pacific.* West Chester, Pa.: Schiffer Publishing Ltd., 1986.

_____. *Twilight on the Lighthouses,* Atglen, Pa: Schiffer Publishing, 1996.

Holland, Francis Ross, Jr. *America's Lighthouses: Their Illustrated History Since 1716.* Brattleboro, Vt.: Stephen Greene Press, 1972.

_____. *Great American Lighthouses.* Washington, D.C.: The Preservation Press, 1989.

Lowry, Shannon and Schultz, Jeff. *Northern Lights: Tales of Alaska's Lighthouses and Their Keepers.* Harrisburg, Pa: Stackpole Books, 1992.

Marc, Jacques. *Historic Shipwrecks of Southern Vancouver Island.* Victoria, B.C., Canada: Underwater Archeology Society of British Columbia, 1990.

Marx, Robert. *Shipwrecks of the Western Hemisphere.* New York: David McKay Company, 1971.

McCormick, William Henry. *The Modern Book of Lighthouses, Lifeboats, and Lightships.* London: W. Heinemann, 1913.

Moe, Christine. *Lighthouses and Lightships.* Monticello, Ill.: 1979.

Naush, John M. *Seamarks: Their History and Development.* London: Stanford Maritime, 1895.

Nelson, Sharlene and Ted. *Washington Lighthouses.* Friday Harbor, Wash.: Umbrella Books, 1990.

Scheina, Robert L. "The Evolution of the Lighthouse Tower," *Lighthouses Then and Now* (supplement to the U.S. Coast Guard Commandant's Bulletin).

Shelton-Roberts, Cheryl and Bruce Roberts. *Lighthouse Families.* Birmingham, AL.: Crane Hill Publishers, 1997.

Snow, Edward Rowe. *Famous Lighthouses of America.* New York: Dodd, Mead, 1955.

_____. *Great Gales and Disasters.* New York: Dodd, Mead, 1952.

United States Coast Guard. *Historically Famous Lighthouses.* CG-232, 1986.

West, Victor. *A Guide to Shipwreck Sites Along the Oregon Coast.* North Bend, Oreg.: West and Wells, 1984.

ABOUT THE AUTHORS

BRUCE ROBERTS and his wife, Cheryl, who helped with the research for this book, live on North Carolina's Outer Banks, not far from the Bodie Island Lighthouse. For many years Bruce was Senior Travel Photographer for *Southern Living* magazine. He started his career working as a photographer for newspapers in Tampa, Florida, and Charlotte, North Carolina. He is the recipient of many photography awards, and some of his photos are in the permanent collection of the Smithsonian Institution. Recently Bruce and Cheryl opened the Lighthouse Gallery & Gifts, a store devoted to lighthouse books, artifacts, and collectibles, in Nags Head.

RAY JONES is a freelance writer and publishing consultant living in Surry, a small town on the coast of Maine. He began his writing career working as a reporter for weekly newspapers in Texas. He has served as an editor for Time-Life Books, as founding editor of *Albuquerque Living* magazine, as a senior editor and writing coach at *Southern Living* magazine, and as publisher of Country Roads Press. Ray grew up in Macon, Georgia, where he was inspired by the writing of Ernest Hemingway and William Faulkner.